A Parent's Best Gift

A Parent's Best Gift

A Practical Guide to Passing Faith on to Our Kids

Leanne Cabral

Printed in the United States of America

Published by Author Academy Elite
P.O. Box 43, Powell, OH 43035
www.AuthorAcademyElite.com

ISBN: 1-943526-50-8
ISBN 13: 978-1-943526-50-5

Unless otherwise indicated Scripture quotations are from the Holy Bible, New International Version ®, NIV ®, Copyright © 1973, 1978, 1984, 2011 by Biblical, Inc. Used by permission of Zondervan. All rights reserved worldwide, www.zondervan.com.

Scripture quotations marked ESV are taken from the Holy Bible, English Standard Version, Copyright © 2001 by Crossway Bibles, a division of Good News Publishers. Used by permission. All rights reserved.

Scripture quotations marked NLT are taken from the Holy Bible, New Living Translation, Copyright © 1996, 2004. Used by permission of Tyndale House Publishers, Inc., Wheaton, Illinois. All rights reserved.

Scripture quotations from THE MESSAGE. Copyright © by Eugene H. Peterson 1993, 1994, 1995, 1996, 2000, 2001, 2002. Used by permission of NavPress. All rights reserved. Represented by Tyndale House Publishers, Inc.

Leanne's work on *A Parent's Best Gift* is a lovely and practical hike through parenting by way of the Fruit of the Spirit. Tenderly, insightfully, vulnerably, she meets parenting readers with chapters buoyed by gracious encouragement and God's faithful goodness.

Tim Huff

Best-selling Author of several books for adults and children,
Director of Youth Unlimited's Compassion Series
compassionseries.com/about/tim-huff

I read this book wishing I had it 20 years ago! Leanne Cabral has written a brutally honest account of her journey as a parent. She gives us permission to accept our humanity and know that this is the toughest assignment we will ever have. Is there anything that rocks our world like our babies? They don't come with a manual.

Well, now you have one! We need real answers and Leanne gives them to us. Her gut level disclosure of her own struggle that led to a deep search for solutions is what makes this such an easy read. The practical applications, strategies and opportunities for self-awareness and intentional parenting is going to change you!

Your legacy will be greater. Your family will be enriched and you'll find yourself handing this book down to your own children.

Laura-Lynn Tyler Thompson

Author "Relentless Redemption"
Co-Host The 700 Club Canada
lauralynn.tv

Strong nations are built on strong foundations. Strong foundations are forged by strong leaders who all have a family of origin that helped establish their values and allow opportunities to learn through adversity. Strong families launch young men and women into their churches, communities, and their country to make them better.

None of the strength of the individual, or the church, or the community comes by accident. It is built intentionally in the home, by parents who are imparting wisdom from the only true source – the Creator and Sustainer of all. Parents who parent intentionally and help guide their children to acknowledge God early on in a personal relationship are partnering in the work of forging a better tomorrow.

Leanne has chosen to impart wisdom in one of the areas most needed in today's culture. She raises the value of parenting, of family, and of being faith-focused, in a culture that says you are better on your own. It takes a village and villages consist of healthy and functional faith-filled families. Leanne focuses not only on principles but practicality in this rich offering called *A Parent's Best Gift*.

Cathie Ostapchuk
Co-Founder, Gather Women
cathieostapchuk.com
gatherwomen.com

It's been an incredible joy for me to pray for and encourage Leanne as she has stepped in to her calling to minister to families. Humble, gracious, tender-hearted and oh-so-wise–Leanne is the real deal. She lives and breaths her faith in all of it's messy, authentic, gorgeous glory. This book, *A Parent's Best Gift*, is the outpouring of her faith journey as a mother, wife and daughter of the most High King. Beautifully written, with personal stories so humbly shared, this book is a masterful blend of wisdom, encouragement and practical guidance on how to pass your faith on to future generations. If you're a parent, grand-parent, coach, or mentor of the next generation, be sure to pick up a copy of this book! It is an absolute treasure!

Dr. Merry C Lin
Psychologist, Speaker and Author of "The Fully Lived Life: Rescuing our Souls from All that Holds Us Back"
drmerrylin.com

Vulnerable, practical and Biblical. Three things I love in a book. In *A Parent's Best Gift,* Leanne shares from herself, her family and her faith of how to pass our faith on to our kids. Great read for parents of kids of all ages.

Brett Ullman
Executive Director: Worlds Apart
brettullman.com

Leanne is a gifted writer and speaker with a passion to see many families following Jesus whole-heartedly! Her workshops and book, *A Parent's Best Gift* are full of practical–doable ideas to help parents with what can feel like a daunting task. She brings inspiration and hope to those that may feel that they have failed. Leanne is a breath of fresh air. She speaks with grace and laughter. This book is a must read in helping you with a plan to see your family growing in faith–together!

Lorie Hartshorn
Pastor, Speaker and Author of "Finding Freedom"
loriehartshorn.com

Dedication

To James, you will always be my most favourite gift~I love pointing our kids to Jesus with you!

To Hannah, Caleb, Ella and Seth, you are the miraculous gifts God used as the catalyst for this remarkable journey~I adore you!

Contents

Welcome

Dear reader ~ I am honoured to be with you and grateful that you have entrusted me with a few minutes of your time. It is a privilege I don't take lightly! May you feel welcome and at home here, like we are sharing a conversation over a hot cup of coffee. Know there is always room for you and a place for you at the table!

There are a few things I want you to know before we start our time together…

You are Invaluable

You are a big deal, just in case you forgot! You are significant, cherished and deeply loved. There is no better person to embark on this journey than you. I firmly believe that you want the very best for your kids and that you want to parent to the best of your ability. I imagine you are doing a pretty awesome job, even when it doesn't feel like it. No one knows your kids better, loves them more or has invested in them as much as you have. The role you play in your child's life is priceless – thank you!

There is No Such Thing as The Perfect Family

Despite what the lovely Christmas card photos portray, and the beautiful social media pictures show, no family is perfect and all families struggle.

Every Family is Broken

We do our very best, but we are all sinful. We came into this world broken and in need of a Saviour. This means we enter into every other relationship broken, including that of family and parenting.

The Face of Family is Always Changing

We have nuclear families. We have single parents raising kids on their own or sharing custody. We have grandparents or aunts and uncles raising grandchildren and nieces and nephews. We have blended and step families, adoptive and foster families. You may be single and have created a chosen family of your own with friends and loved ones. What I want you to know is that ALL families matter to God.

Make it Your Own

Many of the stories you are about to read come from the context of my experience with my own family. Your kids may be older or younger. Your life experience may be very different than mine. You might be parenting on your own or maybe you and your spouse aren't on the same page with some of this stuff. That's ok and you are most welcome here. For others of you, you may not have kids yet. Maybe you teach kids or care for other people's kids. You might serve in kids' ministry or have nieces and nephews or grandchildren that you want to pour into. Please apply the information in this book to your unique situation. Tailor it to your specific needs and make it your own.

Chew on the Meat, Spit out the Bones

You many not agree with all that I share with you in this book. I want you to know that I am totally okay with that and I hope you are too. I love how St. Augustine puts it: "In essentials unity, in non-essentials liberty, in all things charity." What I am asking of you is this, take what makes sense to you in this season of your life and use it as you see fit. What you don't need or want, let it fall by the wayside. My good friend, Brett Ullman puts it this way: "Chew on the meat and spit out the bones."

I am not claiming to know it all and you will quickly discover that I certainly don't have it all together or figured out. I want to share with you some of the things that have made sense to me and what I have learned on this crazy journey of figuring out how to make an invisible faith, visible and tangible to my kids.

Know that I have been praying for you and your family. My desire is to make your load a little lighter. May this task of passing faith on to your kids feel doable and a little less daunting. My hope is that you walk away from our time together feeling embraced, encouraged, excited and equipped for all that the Lord has in store for your family!

Foreword

What if you could give your child the perfect gift? A perfect gift transcends expectations, never breaks, and withstands the test of time.

Leanne Cabral has a passion for equipping parents as they navigate the awesome task of passing faith on to their children. She encourages parents to make their invisible faith tangible so they can intentionally point their kids to Jesus and build a legacy of enduring faith. Leanne is the creator of Bringing Faith Home speaking series, whose mission is to empower ordinary parents to lead extraordinary families.

Leanne believes the best gift we can give our kids is to live our lives in such a way that they know who Jesus is and understand His incredible love for them. While many understand this task in *theory*, most of us struggle practically applying this in everyday life.

A Parent's Best Gift reveals this process, equipping parents with tools and strategies that are simple, applicable, and absolutely doable. Discover freedom, direction, and intentionality as you begin to see this magnificent task broken down into manageable bite-size pieces.

Leanne believes we all want to be the parents God has called us to be and cultivate a faith in our kids that takes root and grows.

Journey with her as she candidly explores the obstacles that entangled her and the clarity that emerged by charting a course of faithfulness for her family. Uncover the significance of intentional living and find freedom with practical activities that are tried, tested and true.

Kary Oberbrunner
CEO of Redeem the Day and Igniting Souls. Co-founder of Author Academy Elite.

Author of *Day Job to Dream Job*, *The Deeper Path*, and *Your Secret Name*.

Part 1

THE GIFT GIVEN...

Freedom

F our littles, still in their pyjamas, were strapped snug in their carseats. The predawn light just beginning to chase the night away. The van was overflowing with all that a family of six needed for a two-week vacation, including a roof-top carrier bursting at the seams with all the "must-have" beach accessories. Movies and books were selected and each child had their own custom-made survival pack for our 28-hour journey that would take place over the next two days. The excitement was palpable as we embarked on our first family road trip to Fort Lauderdale, Florida.

Some people are all about the journey. They research and meticulously plan out their routes. They determine the best places to stop, eat and stretch their legs. They love discovering quaint spots to explore and linger. They search for historical landmarks and all the "must-sees" and "must-do's" so that their family can experience the fullness of their adventure.

We are not that family. As much as I want to be about the journey, if I am honest, I am totally destination-driven. I feel there is no need to stop unless the gas tank is empty. My approach to life is very similar. I like to meet a task or a goal head on, and I delight in finding the most effective and efficient way to do something. It drives my husband crazy.

If you are like me and just want to get on with it, this first part of the book might frustrate you a little. But if I am to tell this story accurately and authentically, I must tell you about the obstacles. I have to include the parts where the Lord interrupted my quest, forcing me to stop and linger. My goal for embarking on this journey, was to figure out the practical part of passing on a faith to my kids that would stick and take root. I understood the theory, but I didn't know how to make my invisible faith visible and tangible to my kids in the midst of the chaos of everyday life. Though my aim was to figure this out, the Lord's plans were clearly a little different. His plans seemed to be more about the hurdles that entangled me. Little did I know what a joy these obstacles would become. I soon came to realize that by leaning into them, the gift I was being given was my own *freedom*… one inconvenient hurdle at a time.

Chapter 1

Full Bloom Parenting

The gentle breeze only seemed to intensify as I swung upward. Pumping my legs harder and harder I began to soar higher and higher. It was a balmy, end-of-summer kind of day. Whimsical clouds that were cotton ball fluffy, danced across the sapphire sky. I was in a new place on my favourite swing.

I loved the feeling of soaring higher and the tickle in my tummy that made me giggle out loud. As far as my six-year-old eyes could see in front of me, there were beautiful golden wheat fields ready for harvest. The wind blew through them like ocean waves coming and going. I liked this new place.

My dad came outside that morning and asked if I would like to join him on an errand. I was secretly hoping it might end at the "SS". I didn't realize then that it stood for the "Service Station" by the highway. To me, it was the place where my dad washed the floors at night and where they made the biggest, stickiest, most delicious homemade cinnamon buns. He held out his hand and I placed mine in his and we began to walk together. I loved holding my dad's hand, rubbing my little fingers over his textured wedding band that reminded me of tree bark. I don't recall what we talked about that morning but I know my hand was tucked safely inside his, and I remember feeling like I was the only thing that mattered to him that day.

I watched my dad chat and laugh with the other students as we all waited in a very long line that snaked along a few curves. I remember looking up at my dad and asking him what we were doing here. He smiled and said it was time to pay for his classes. While we passed the time it was obvious to me that these people were drawn to my dad. I knew, even then, that people liked him and I loved being known as Hans' daughter. At the front of the line sat a lady behind a table with a clipboard and a metal box. She smiled at us and asked for my dad's name.

"Hans Hamer" he said, "or it might be under Johannes Hamer." I watched her adjust her glasses and check through the stack of papers in front of her. She smiled and looked up: "Here you are."

"Great," my dad replied. "How much do I owe you?" he asked, reaching for his wallet. She laughed and said, "Well nothing, Hans. It seems your tuition has already been paid."

"What?" my dad said as he began to laugh. "Are you sure?"

"Yes," she reassured him. I could see a tear running down his cheek as he continued to laugh. "I am not really sure what to say," he gasped. He looked at me and then at the lady, showing us his empty wallet and said, "I was trying to figure out what to tell you once I got to the front of the line. I knew I didn't have the money to pay for this and I was hoping I could convince you to let me enrol anyway." She slapped her leg, threw her head back and released a deep belly laugh. "So you have no idea who paid this?" she asked.

"Not a clue," he laughed, as they both continued to tear up and giggle.

I can't remember if we ever made it to the SS that morning, but God's provision that day will be forever engrained in my memory. Though this is the first time I remember seeing God's provision so tangibly, it certainly wasn't the last. I had a front row seat to God's care and faithfulness to us all the time. You see, I grew up in a family where they took following Jesus pretty seriously. My parents quit their jobs as a police officer and bank teller. They sold their split-level suburban home, packed up their two kids, threw their earthly belongings into a station wagon and small trailer, then headed off to Bible College. They both sensed the Lord calling them into full-time ministry as missionaries in The Netherlands. My parents' faith cost them something; their obedience had a price tag. Now I have the privilege of living in the legacy and blessing of that obedience.

I tell you this story because if anyone should have been able to figure out how to make her invisible faith visible and tangible to her kids, it should have been me. I had parents in full-time ministry, I grew up on the mission field and I got to see faith lived out first-hand. I saw God provide for us over and over again. Yet once I found myself in the midst of parenting and living out my own faith, I felt at a complete loss. I knew that it was something I wanted to do well. I felt the weight of this responsibility and I knew that I would be held accountable for how I did this. I couldn't shake off the pressure and it only intensified with each baby that became a part of our family.

I understood the *theory* of passing faith on to our kids, but where

I felt completely ill-equipped was with the *practical*, *"how-to"* piece. The church and other Christian resources did a great job talking about the importance of pointing our kids to Jesus, but the *"how-to"* conversation, seemed to be missing. I began to share this growing concern with other parents hoping they could point me in the right direction, but it quickly became clear I was not the only one feeling this way. The application that I was so desperate for, seemed to be absent. I soon discovered that parents who had come from a legacy of faith as well as those who had just met Jesus, felt the same longing and burden.

I found myself at a crossroad—too discontent to stay where I was, yet not knowing how to move forward. The problem was, I couldn't seem to find the answers I was seeking, I also couldn't silence the growing whisper inside telling me to keep looking— it was quickly becoming louder. It was in this odd place of the unknown where I decided to lean in and research this for myself. I wanted to see what others were doing—to learn how other families were making their faith tangible in their home. I was compelled to figure this out so I could more effectively live out my own faith before my kids and teach them to do the same. Psalm 78: 1-7 captured the groaning of my heart so well.

> *"My people, hear my teaching; listen to the words of my mouth.*
>
> *I will open my mouth with a parable; I will utter hidden things, things from of old, things we have heard and known, things our ancestors have told us.*
>
> *We will not hide them from their descendants; we will tell*

the next generation the praiseworthy deeds of the Lord, his power, and the wonders he has done.

He decreed statutes for Jacob and established the law in Israel which he commanded our ancestors to teach their children,

So the next generation would know them, even the children yet to be born, and they in turn would tell their children.

Then they would put their trust in God and would not forget his deeds but would keep his commands."[1]

As I began this new journey, I was surprised at how quickly I became entangled in my own obstacles. I started thinking about my role as a parent and what my job description looked like. My considerable list included words like caregiver, teacher, nurse, chauffeur, personal shopper, comforter, problem solver, pastor, referee, baker, cook, maid, coach, comedian, social convener, event planner, entertainer… just to name a few. The more I looked at that list the more disheartened I felt—who wouldn't feel a little overwhelmed? I had to start rethinking expectations—the expectations I had of myself and the expectations I felt from others.

EXPECTATIONS

I became pregnant with Hannah at 23 and though I wouldn't have said this out loud, I thought parenting would come pretty easy to me. I figured I had the basic skill set to navigate my way through. Not much freaked me out or had me concerned; I was pretty calm, collected and in control. I soon realized parenting was a lot of work, and while I appeared to be managing on the outside, it was bringing out both the best and the worst in me. I had heartwarming, romantic, "rose-coloured glasses" kind of expectations, and it was becoming clear that those expectations might be a little askew.

Full Bloom Parenting

I thought parenting was something at which I would excel. I began to understand there are few things that we are instantly good at doing. Most of us have to work pretty hard and spend a lot of time practising to master something, and even then we aren't necessarily brilliant at it. Looking back I can see that I was a much better mother to my youngest, Seth, as an infant, than I was to my eldest, Hannah, at the same stage. You see, I had figured out a few things by the time he came along. I had some practise and experience under my belt, having benefitted from six years worth of trial and error with three other babies. There is no such thing as full bloom parenting—we learn it moment by moment.

We come into this role of parent in our brokenness. We have our own baggage, our own hurts and experiences, expectations and assumptions, hopes and dreams. We are sinful and we have an enemy who strategically works against us. And yet, we are often surprised when things don't play out as we planned. We are heartbroken when we fail or mess things up.

Hard on Ourselves

We can be so hard on ourselves. We know our own shortcomings all too well and we have an enemy who delights in reminding us of them. Scripture calls him "the accuser."

We also have a habit of looking at others who seem to make it look so easy. We are bombarded by "perfect" social media images and super-fun tweets or status updates and before we know it, we begin to compare our everyday lives to someone else's highlight reel. Comparison is subtle and it creeps in so deviously. It often swallows us up before we even realize it, and it breeds discontent.

Sometimes we find ourselves trying to meet the expectations others place upon us—what they think good parenting and well-behaved kids look like. It might be a friend, neighbour or even your own family. I was starting to see that I was trying to please everyone else and do what they said was right. I was judging myself and my parenting ability on the snapshot I saw of someone else's life; living under the perceived judgment of others, which often left me feeling inadequate.

Hard on Each Other
Truthfully, as parents we can be quick to judge or draw conclusions. The trouble is, we often judge our own parenting and that of others based on how the kids are behaving. This strategy works great if you have a compliant child, because they will always make you look brilliant and reflect you well. It is then so hard to understand a spirited child, or one who wrestles with eating or sleeping, or one struggling with separation anxiety, all because this just isn't *our* experience.

What works well for each of us only works because of the unique combination of personalities and temperaments in our homes; each family has its own recipe. It isn't our job to judge ourselves or others. This is the Holy Spirit's task. When we step into that role, we also step into sin that will need to be confessed. We have to trust God to be the judge of us and that He, like a good shepherd, will faithfully call us back when we wander.

We have an incredible opportunity to come alongside each other—especially those who are having a more difficult time. We have a chance to breathe life, grace and love while we support each other. We need each other because we are divinely designed for community. We are created in the image of the Almighty God, who in His very nature is three-in-one community. Don't believe the lie that you can do it on your own or that you are a burden. Lean into community; you were made for it. Generously breathe words of life and encouragement into others.

I didn't expect this journey to start with me. I was excited to research what others were doing and how they were living out their faith in their homes. I was pursuing information and how to apply it. But, in His typical God-like fashion, He began with what matters most to Him… His own child. He started with *me*. His primary focus will always be the internal workings of our hearts.

Like a good dad, He lovingly shows us the lies that entangle us *and* the truth that releases us into all that He has called us to. It's easy for us to become preoccupied with the fruit that our lives yield, but He is forever tending to our roots—how deep and how wide they are growing. It is an invisible kind of work, but healthy roots always yield great harvests. This journey of equipping you to pass faith onto your kids needs to start with you and your roots. The fields are ripe unto harvest and we will trust the Lord of the Harvest to nurture our roots and multiply our fruit.

My dad had no idea how much that invitation to join him on that early morning errand would affect me and my faith journey. He had no clue that his bold obedience in response to the Father's call would not only impact his family, but countless others too. He built a legacy of faith, one simple act of obedience at a time. Please know that your seemingly mundane choices of daily obedience are building a legacy too. I didn't know what a gift this "burden" would become—trying to figure out how to make an invisible faith visible to my kids. My primary motivation was my kids' faith—it was for their freedom. I had no idea that by leaning into it, I was actually beginning to unwrap my own *freedom* as well.

EMBRACING THE GIFT

A Moment to Reflect

- What aspects of parenting do you do well?
- What aspects of parenting would you like to do differently?
- What is one thing you could do to invite community into your journey?
- What is one thing you could do to breathe life into another parent?
- As you read this first chapter, what is the Holy Spirit stirring within you?

Chapter 2

Death to Comparison

Have you ever had a morning where you wake up before the kids and you actually feel rested? You decide to get up and savour a tantalizing cup of warm heavenly deliciousness and spend a few moments of quiet with the Lord before embarking on the busyness of the day. Then kids wake up, surprisingly happy, and your morning routine is notably less rushed and turbulent than normal. The kids are getting along and though you could clean up the breakfast dishes, you choose to take a quick glance at your social media accounts, curious as to what the rest of the world is up to today. You begin to scroll through your feed and before you know it 15 minutes has been poached, along with your calm and content morning. Suddenly you find yourself needing new granite counter tops, bewildered at how it is possible that you still have white appliances. You question why you didn't bake muffins or make the kids' lunches in fancy, new, perfectly sectioned bento boxes. You are compelled to fill your calendar with playdates and adventurous new outings and you feel an abrupt urge to buy a little blackboard frame for the kids' first day of school. What was seemingly peaceful and serene has been hijacked by "what the heck am I doing?" and "we need a life" and "under achievers 'R' us." Discontentment sucker-punches you and flips your gratifying life, of a moment ago, upside down.

I love social media and it's boundless potential. It has allowed me to connect with friends old and new from all over the world that I never thought I'd see again. It has made my world smaller and yet bigger. I don't understand how it all works but I love it and hate it at the same time. It brings me great joy as well as deep sadness. It evokes both celebration and envy in me. It is a contradiction to me, and I wrestle with the perks and pitfalls of it. In this quest to figure out how faith is tangibly lived out, the Lord was continuing to show me the obstacles that entangled me and *comparison* came forth as a big flashing neon sign.

A scarcity mindset subtly began to creep in. Thoughts around not being enough or not having enough often danced through my mind; waltzing into my attitude, emotions and choices. Discontentment was palpable. The quest for more was alluring, and the desire to show my wins, enticing. They all were birthed from this place of comparison. Nauseated by this, I knew I needed to learn how to rewire my thoughts and align my behaviour. I wanted to find a new way to interact with social media, one where I wouldn't be a conduit of wanting, perpetuating the same lies that entangled me. I wanted to create space virtually and in real life, where I could live authentically and less filtered. My desire was for my life and my online space to be congruent and authentic, where abundant thinking runs free and where everything is seasoned with humility, honesty and grace.

CONTENTMENT

While exploring the topic of contentment, I stumbled upon an incredible podcast series by Craig Groeschel[1], and much of what you are about to read are his insights that deeply resonated with me.

"Never before have we had so much and yet want so much more. Researchers did a study at two college universities, and they had students spend half an hour on Facebook, and then surveyed their feelings after half an hour of just looking at Facebook. And what they found was, one third of the students felt significantly depressed, citing envy as the number one emotion of what they felt, after 30 minutes of just watching what happens on Facebook."[2]

Envy can play out in many facets of our lives, not only in social media. Envy is wanting what I do not have or comparing what I don't have to what you do have. No one wins when we compare, yet we all do it. Knowingly or unknowingly we check each other out and measure. We make judgements and assumptions. Wanting what we do not have is coveting. This is an ancient struggle that goes right back to the Garden of Eden. Eve too wanted something she didn't have. What I love about this is that God in His infinite wisdom knew that His kids would be lured by this need to compare and covet, so in His mercy He included it for generation upon generation in the Ten Commandments.

Exodus 20:17

"You shall not covet your neighbour's house. You shall not covet your neighbour's wife, or his male or female servant, his ox or donkey, or anything that belongs to your neighbour."[3]

Meditating on this verse, *coveting* or wanting what we do not have seems to fall into three areas: wanting someone else's *possessions*, wanting their *people*, and wanting their *position* in life.

Possessions—Wanting More Things

One warm spring afternoon I sat on my Muskoka chair and flipped through a magazine. Two kids were laughing behind me, swinging on their play set. The other two were blowing bubbles and painting the fence with brushes and water. I was reading an article about a family who chose to do a shopping fast. For two months they decided that they would buy nothing but groceries and the occasional gift when their son was invited to a birthday party. The author explained that the family decided this, not because they were struggling financially, but because they felt convicted about their consumerism and the message of materialism they were sending to their son. Contentment, comparing and coveting were at the forefront of my mind those days and this article struck a deep chord with me. I felt the Holy Spirit's beckoning to give this a try.

My husband, James, and I decided that for the entire summer, our family would buy nothing but groceries and the occasional birthday gift for a friend. It was tough! When you have four kids under seven, the mall is a free, sensory-stimulating, air-conditioned place to hang out. We would stop at the pet store, watch a few songs on the Gymboree TV, wander through the toy store and, just like that, two hours would disappear. I began to see my own consumerism and wanting in high definition. The lure to buy was palpable, especially if it was on sale. What surprised me most was that I was content at home, not longing for anything. But once I entered that building I was suddenly confronted by all the "must-have" things I didn't even know I wanted. A month earlier, I would have picked up the clearance $5 jeans without even thinking... the ones I didn't even want until I saw them for $5. I found satisfaction in the deal. Shopping solicited discontentment, and $5 deals summoned coveting. The Lord was answering me, showing me exactly where coveting possessions was playing out in my heart and in my hands.

Neighbours' porches were adorned with beautiful cascading mini wave petunias and I was smitten, but I tucked that want away because we were committed to this fast. Inside our house my gaze would often turn to an old, outdated country table that sat in front of the window in the family room. It was long out of style and yearning to be replaced. I chose to look away, as this was not the season for acquiring possessions, but rather a time to abstain.

The bold display of His generosity during this fast was something I didn't expect to see. One morning while I was heading out with the kids, I noticed something pink tucked in with my neighbour's garbage. I had to stop by for a closer look and to my surprise, it was a pink mini wave petunia they were throwing away. It was growing a little wonky and leaned to the left, but I didn't care. My plan was to put it on a shelf and let it cascade down the fence. It was stunning! For an entire summer, a breathtaking waterfall of pink, lush flowers descended down my fence, pooling on to the grass beneath it. Interestingly, I have bought one every year since then and I have never had one that ever did that again!

A few weeks later, the kids and I were coming home from a friend's place, and as I drove into our subdivision a wooden table caught my attention. It was nestled between two garbage bags. I stopped the van, pulled it out, dusted it off and I was instantly enamoured by it. It was a beautiful, ornate old dressing table, a perfect replacement for that old country one in front of the window.

I was struck at the Father's extravagance in all of this. He didn't have to provide for either one of those desires, since they certainly weren't needs. But He did. Just like we love giving our kids unexpected gifts, so our Heavenly Father delights in giving His children surprises too. As He was teaching me about my own struggle with contentment and the allure to covet, He was simultaneously displaying another side of His love for me and His delight in giving His kids gifts too.

People—Wanting Other People's Relationships

This is a tricky one, right? When I was growing up the only way you knew you were left out was when you rode your bike by a friend's house and saw all the other bikes parked out on the driveway. Today you can instantly and continuously find out all that you have not been included in or invited to on social media. Perhaps you have experienced taking your kids to the park or to school and you see the other parents interacting. You want to join in and feel that sense of belonging, but you hesitate as they all seem to have their "go-to" people. No one likes to be left out and we all know what it feels like when you are. It is hard to see friendships play out when you feel alone or overlooked. It is complicated when you want to join in and be a part of something, and everyone already seems to have "their" people. We are drawn to the snippets of how things appear versus the actual reality. Like a good beer commercial, we are enticed by these snapshots of friendships with people who appear to be happy and having the time of their lives!

Sometimes it's not so much the friendships we covet, but marriages or family life. Seeing someone else's husband doting on their wife can be like salt in a wound when your marriage is struggling. As I write this, it's back-to-school week for us and while my social media feed was saturated with celebratory parents and smiling kids on their first day of school, I dropped my 13-year-old off to her first day of high school in tears. Wires had gotten crossed and her friend was late and now she was terrified to enter the great unknown of high school alone. I fought back my own tears as I gave her my best pep talk, desperately trying to convince her that she would be okay. Courageously, with a tear-stained face, she exited the van and walked towards her biggest fear. I spent the rest of the morning crying and interceding for her—a stark contrast to the images on Facebook that I so wanted to be our experience.

As kids, most of us had to guess if we were popular or not—today you can actually measure it. It is measured by the amount of comments you get on your Facebook status. It is seen in the number of likes you get on your Instagram photos. It is celebrated by retweets and shared posts.

Craig Groeschel continues in his podcast series: "We as a society have become addicted to 'likes' and immediate personal affirmation, instant gratification and feedback. Scientists say that every time we share something and it is 'liked,' dopamine is released into the body and we experience the high. We, as a society, are becoming addicted to dopamine and the high that it gives."[4]

Are we beginning to substitute real relationships for virtual ones? It is enticing to do friendship on our own terms. I can show you the "me" that I want to portray because I can edit my post as many times as I need so that it says exactly what I want. I can filter my photo in such a way that it will show you exactly what I want you to see. Are we doing relationships from a safe distance, while neglecting getting messy and involved?

Though we are made in the image of the Almighty God, who in His very nature is three-in-one community, we want light, easy, clean community. Real relationships are sloppy and sometimes uncomfortable; as believers, we are called to embrace each other and walk together. When tragedy strikes, it might be easier to respond by text or a Facebook acknowledgement as most of us don't know what to say, how to behave or what to do. This is a great first step, but let's follow up with our presence too. Don't forget that as believers, we have the indwelling of the Holy Spirit. There is power in simply being there, even when we have no idea what to say or do, because where two or three are gathered I AM is there. Our very presence is comfort because of the Holy Spirit in us.

Position—Wanting Other People's Lot in Life

Honestly, I think we all fantasize about what it would be like to live someone else's life. However, for some it goes beyond innocent imagination. Thoughts like "I hoped I'd be pregnant by now" or "I expected we'd own our own house by now" play in our mind. Or maybe these sound familiar: "I thought we'd be stable financially" or "Wouldn't it be nice if we got to go on a cruise every year too." This form of envy is a short dark road paved by hurt that always leads to discontentment.

Two years ago, James, the sole income earner for our family, was unexpectedly laid off. The company declared bankruptcy and his severance package never materialized. He spent six months unemployed and when he began his new job, he took a 40%

pay cut. I was thrilled he had a job, but I wrestled with this new reality. We were living on less than we did when we got married 19 years earlier, with four more dependants. I felt like we had been sent back to start. It was hard not to look around at other families at the same age and stage as us and compare, but I knew that if I lingered there discontentment would envelop me.

Coveting and envy are birthed from an emptiness that demands to be filled. A space we try to pacify with things, people, approval and accomplishments, only to discover that it doesn't last, it only satisfies for a moment. We have a built-in longing for something more than this world has to offer and it is Jesus. He is the secret to contentment. He alone can fill our deepest need for love, value and purpose. We can have all the material possessions we'd like, deep meaningful relationships, an impressive position in life, but unless God fills that space, we will always long for something more—and we will continue to soothe it with things that leave us empty.

PRACTICAL THOUGHTS

Guard Your Heart

Could it be time for a social media fast? You might be feeding coveting unknowingly as you scroll though your social media feeds. Maybe you need to block an account that evokes feelings of want and discontentment. It might be the Pottery Barn catalogue that causes you to feel unsatisfied with what you have—throw it out. You, like me, may need a shopping fast to refocus your thinking so that you can be happy with what you already have. Others may need to turn off Home and Garden TV because of the envy it elicits.

Practise Gratitude

"Envy is resenting God's goodness in someone else's life and ignoring His goodness in our own life."[5] Start celebrating the successes of others. Often we wait for our emotions to agree with our actions before we decide something. Psychologists have been telling us for years that when emotions are high, logic shuts down. If we wait to feel something before we decide to do what is right, it may never happen. As believers we must engage our will first, and then ask the Lord to align our emotions to His will. Ask the Lord to purify our motives so that our choices are made from a place of authenticity. Imagine using our social media feed as an opportunity to pray for our friends and family and to thank the Lord for their successes? What if we choose to respond in celebration and words of blessing when jealousy creeps up, congratulating the wins of others in real life and online? Perhaps starting and ending our day with three things that we are thankful for is a way of acknowledging His goodness in our own life and refocusing our thoughts.

Opportunity

Whether you realize it or not, you are marketing you and your values on your social media space. You have the privilege of creating virtual space that is vastly different from the average person. We are a selfie-obsessed culture that reveals who we are through specifically chosen, filtered images. Craig Groeschel warns us "The more filtered our lives become the more difficult it is to be authentic. While we impress people with our strengths, we connect with them through our weaknesses."[6] What an incredible opportunity to leverage virtual space as a life-giving conduit, making it authentic and others-focused. Champion others and align it to your unique values.

You are fearfully and wonderfully made. You are deeply loved, unique and made in the image of the Almighty God. You are created for community and relationships. It is in your very DNA, so get messy. Fill that longing for more than this world has to offer with Jesus and fight the urge to appease it with prestige, people and things. Scripture exhorts us to hold every thought captive (2 Corinthians 10:5). Controlling a first thought may prove difficult, but you certainly get to choose your second. People are drawn to contentment and they will be drawn to the peace it leaves in you. Accordingly, it will draw them to the Prince of Peace.

"Above all else, guard your heart, for everything you do flows from it" (Proverbs 4:23).[7] Discontent was where I was, comparing brought me there, but contentment was where I wanted to be. I didn't know how to get there. The Lord gently began to show me the specific areas of my life where comparison and coveting lived. The Holy Spirit allowed me to feel unsettled when my thoughts headed towards scarcity. Discontentment began to loosen and I started doing things differently. As He disentangled comparison, I began to unwrap the gift of contentment. Another layer of *freedom* was given and He showed me how to guard my heart in a consumer-crammed, selfie-saturated world.

EMBRACING THE GIFT

- What is stirring within you after reading this?
- Where is comparison or discontentment present in your life?
- What do your social media accounts say about you?
- Do you need to make any changes to align your virtual space with your values?
- Are there any practical steps you need to take or any safeguards to implement to root out comparison?

Chapter 3

Warped Views

Three excited children bounced up the stairs to welcome our visitors on the other side of the door. Delighted to have a new friend to play with, they greeted our guests with hugs, smiles and cheers. A family from church was joining us for dinner. We didn't know them well, but I was drawn to them and wanted to know them more.

Squeals of laughter came from the basement as new friends quickly became fast friends. Adults exchanged polite conversation at first, but quickly dove into deeper, richer content. The mom shared her journey of taking a sabbatical from teaching to pursue a master's degree, as she felt the Lord was calling her into something more. She was studying to become a Spiritual Director and while that sounded a little New Age to this conservative girl, I was intrigued. She explained that spiritual direction was a relationship centred around prayer with the purpose of drawing near to the Spirit of God. It is about the process of spiritual transformation, seeking the Lord together, through prayer and Scripture and following the Holy Spirit's promptings.

Her final assignment was to lead a six-session spiritual direction group. She had one participant and needed at least one more. I had observed her closely the last few months. Her faith was real and vibrant. She was deeply rooted in the truth of the gospel and desperately loved Jesus. Her passion to help others recognize the voice of God for themselves was palpable. She delighted in coming alongside others, bearing witness to their healing and freedom as they walked in the Truth.

Before I could take back the words, I heard myself volunteering. I was clueless to the life-transforming journey I was about to embark on, oblivious to the truth and freedom that was just around the bend. The Lord in His mercy was continuing to show me the obstacles that entangled me… even the ones I didn't know existed.

WARPED VIEW OF MYSELF

The problem with a warped view is that you don't even know it's warped—it feels like truth to you because it is all that you know. I didn't know I had this view of myself. I knew I had some negative self-talk and that my head was noisy sometimes. But I thought that it was normal and something everyone experienced.

I knew my shortcomings well, as did the enemy who delighted in reminding me of them. Condemning thoughts like "What makes you think you are a good mom?" or "Are you sure you're not going to mess up these kids?" often cut through my mind. Accusations like "How can you possibly raise kids to love Jesus if you are their example?" and "You and your kids are what gives Christians a bad name" flowed frequently.

Ephesians 2 states that there are three voices that compete against the voice of God. The apostle Paul refers to them as the *flesh, the world* and *the devil.* We still deal with those voices today. Our own voice—our internal thinking and rationalization. The voice of others—words spoken by family, friends, coworkers and the media. The voice of the enemy—satan and his demons.

My head was often loud and all three of those voices were familiar to me. The enemy worked tirelessly trying to convince me that I wasn't enough and that I had nothing of value to contribute. Simultaneously, I felt this palpable longing to be a part of something greater than myself, an inward yearning for more, a nagging restlessness. I longed to be part of a much bigger story, one where an ordinary person takes on an extraordinary challenge. As the enemy tried to convince me of my insignificance, God was pursuing me and placing longings in my heart for the call He placed on my life.

Apprehensively I went to my first spiritual direction session. As we prayed and listened, the Lord affectionately revealed His thoughts toward me. Each session delicately exposed a little more. Through Scripture, He spoke about the plans He had for me. In contrast to the turbulence in my head, He whispered soothing truths about my value and worth. Truth often embraced by tears as it penetrated such tender places… the gravity of which was almost unbearable at times. This was a healing process of renewing my mind and my spirit (Ephesians 4:23)—identifying the accusations of the enemy and rebuking him, just as Jesus did when He was tempted in the wilderness. I began to recognize my own self-talk when it deviated from the Truth. This warped view of myself could no longer stay hidden—it was clearly exposed and the Lord was renewing and rewiring my mind with His Truth.

WARPED VIEW OF GOD

I knew that God loved me—I never questioned that, but I always felt like He was slightly disappointed in me. Images of Him shaking His head, saying "Come on, Leanne, you can do so much better than this" often swirled through my thoughts. I felt I couldn't measure up to His expectations or plans for me, like I wasn't good enough or worthy of being entrusted with things of eternal value. This tainted understanding of God and myself paralyzed me, especially the guilt and fear that accompanied it.

I felt like I was constantly letting my family and God down. I knew my failures well and some of them were big. The enemy revelled in replaying them over and over in my mind. I felt the weight of my responsibility as a mother and for pointing my kids to Jesus. I was so afraid of messing it up. Reading parenting books or attending workshops didn't happen, as I was so afraid of being accused of all that I wasn't doing. Guilt, shame and fear are always an enemy strategy. Condemnation and lies are his mother tongue—but I didn't know that at the time. Scripture says that it is God's *kindness* (Romans 2:4) that leads us to repentance, not shame or guilt.

Sitting on the sofa early one morning, while the kids were still tucked in their beds, I flipped through my Bible. A novelty during a season where so much is vying for your love and attention and time seems to slip through your fingers. I stumbled upon Isaiah 40:11.

> *"He tends his flock like a shepherd:*
> *He gathers the lambs in his arms*

and carries them close to his heart;
he gently leads those that have young."[1]

That last phrase, "gently leads those with young" leapt off the page… I was one of "those with young." I pondered this and what it means to gently lead. Images of my own children learning to walk flooded my mind, fondly remembering their delight and mine, as they courageously took those first few steps. I was so proud of them! I began to see that just as I celebrated each one of their brave steps, the Lord celebrated each one of mine. As I would comfort my children and help them back up when they fell, He also consoled me and gently brought me to firm footing. He took delight in encouraging me to move forward just like I loved cheering my kids on. As I didn't expect my kids to walk at my pace, I was happy to walk at theirs—He too wasn't mad that I couldn't keep up, He patiently met me where I was. When you gently lead someone, it is compassionate, mixed with affection, patience and understanding. This display of God's character began to erase my own warped view of Him.

The unveiling of a warped view begins when someone points it out to you—this was the gift of spiritual direction. In sacred time set aside to listen, the Lord *"allured me into the wilderness and spoke tenderly to me"* (Hosea 2:14). He, like a good dad, reminded me of who I am and what I was created for. As a frightened child finds comfort and safety in the arms of their father, He tended to me and gently scraped away lies I believed and placed the healing balm of Truth on wounded places.

Jeremiah 29 :13 says, *"If you look for me with all your heart, you will find me,"[2]* and this is what happened to me. In my pursuit of faith and how it is lived out in the home, I tumbled into life-transforming Truth. He found me and graciously presented me with my warped understandings and His Truth. The quest to understand how to pass my faith on to my kids continued to be about me and the undoing of traps that ensnared me. It began with expectations and comparison and now warped views were being expunged. Each entanglement exposed another layer of the gift given—*freedom*.

EMBRACING THE GIFT

A Moment to Reflect

- What is stirring within you?
- Is there anything you need to do about it?
- What are the thoughts you hear in your mind when you are still?
- Ask the Holy Spirit to show you the lies—ask Him to root them out and rebuke the lies with His Truth.
- What does Scripture say about you?
- Ask the Holy Spirit what He says about you
- Are there any next steps you need to take to continue to root out lies?
- Is there anything practical you can do to allow His Truth about you to penetrate your mind and heart?

Chapter 4

Embracing the Challenge

Continuing on in the quest to figure out how to tangibly live out my faith before my kids, the Lord seemed to sprinkle unexpected obstructions along the way that demanded my attention before I could keep going. They certainly weren't ones I anticipated and they often felt like overstuffed, weighted down backpacks, overflowing with too much gear—they were heavy, cumbersome and slowed me down, often knocking me to my knees. I was destination driven and I didn't feel like I had a whole lot of disposable time. My goal was to figure this out. I wasn't terribly interested in the scenery along the way—I had an objective and that was my target. These unexpected road blocks frustrated me as they stood between me and my journey's end. Yet God in His infinite wisdom knew that I couldn't move forward without tending to the obstacles that entangled me. Up until this point the journey was primarily about me, my faith and my untangling—I was desperate to get to the next leg of this journey, the one where I could begin to uncover and implement practical tools in making an invisible faith visible. But it was in this place where I was crumbling beneath the weight, that character was being cultivated, lies were being weeded out and hope was beginning to sprout. There was however one more hurdle that the

Lord wanted to address before I continued on—*success*.

"Mom", "Mom", MOM!!" Hannah hollered, as I was frantically trying to get three kids out of the house before 8:30 a.m. I snapped my head around and glared at her, while simultaneously wiping Ella's breakfast off her tiny face. "What!" I replied impatiently. "Caleb, go brush your teeth," I barked, as she stretched out her arm, showing me the large, red rash covering her upper arm. The area where she had her four-year-old needle a few days before was red, hot and inflamed. I had spent the last six hours soothing a fussy baby who was coming down with something and consoling a toddler who had one too many bad dreams. I was tired, frustrated and overwhelmed… and I had to teach a class at 9 a.m.

With bloodshot eyes and tears running down my face I dropped the kids off. Everything within me wanted a re-do of the morning. A morning where I was kind and patient—one where I could stay home and take my kids back to the doctor for a follow up, or that wasn't marked by sharp tones, short words and rushing three littles out the door. How had I gotten to this place? I was drowning, exhausted and completely empty. I had nothing left to give. Crying and venting with the Lord on my way to class, I was suddenly struck by an obvious question: "Why am I doing all this? What am I trying to prove?" With impeccable clarity I heard Him tenderly say, "Leanne, the only thing I hold you responsible for is how you care for your family. I never asked you to do all of this—you chose it."

He was right. My plate was overflowing because of all that I had chosen to put on it. I thought that being a well-rounded, successful woman included caring for my home, raising my kids, building a successful business, serving at my church, being an available friend and an attentive wife. What was clearly emerging out of the chaos was the only piece I wanted to keep on my plate, the only thing I sensed the Lord was asking me to do well was to care for my family and create a safe, warm, peaceful environment at home. That afternoon I began the process of removing the excess from my plate including closing down a successful, booming business. A difficult choice, but one that brought great freedom. I had to learn to redefine success by God's standards, not mine or the world's.

Please know that whether you work inside the home or outside of it, I am for you. Let's celebrate and champion each other as we walk in obedience towards the unique calling God has placed on each one of us. I had to consider a few things and perhaps these questions are of value to you too. Is my identity, worth or value found in what I can do, whether at home or at work? What is the Lord asking of me? Am I willing to let go of being at home or being at work if that is what the Lord asks of me? Friend, what I want you to know is that your inherent value is not based on what you can do, but in the irrational love of God who simply loves you for who you are—a love that does not rise or fall based on your performance. It's a love that cannot be earned or severed, for it is freely given.

SUCCESSFUL PARENTING

Have you ever thought about what it means to be a successful parent—what does successful parenting look like? When I pose this question to a group of parents I often get a mixed response of phrases like, "raising kids who become independent and contribute to society" or "parenting kids with good character."

Others say, "bringing up kids who know and love the Lord." Sprinkled in there are usually great thoughts around "kids who know they are loved and accepted" and "kids who are healthy physically, mentally, emotionally and spiritually."

I follow that question with another—how do we measure success? The room gets pretty quiet at that moment, as the point begins to sink in. Measuring success in parenting is tricky. Typically we measure success based on a pass or fail scale. Yet when you apply that scale to parenting we can't seem to reconcile it. We all know parents who deeply love the Lord, but have kids who aren't walking with Him at the moment. Does that mean that they failed? I think we also all know great Godly people who came from families who haven't met the Lord yet. Calibrating success on a pass or fail scale can only be measured by the kids our parenting produces and how they turn out... Is that fair? Is it accurate?

Let's look at the Bible for a moment, take Hebrews 11—almost all of these people came from severely dysfunctional families, yet they are etched in Biblical history as the Heroes of Faith— which on a side note, gives me great hope! I think the next logical question then becomes—what is God asking of us as parents?

The Bible says...

Deuteronomy 6:6-7

"And you must commit yourselves wholeheartedly to these commands that I am giving you today. Repeat them again and again to your children. Talk about them when you are at home and when you are on the road, when you are going to bed and when you are getting up." [1]

Ephesians 6:4

"Fathers, do not provoke your children to anger by the way you treat them. Rather, bring them up with the discipline and instruction that comes from the Lord."[2]

Proverbs 29:17

"Discipline your children, and they will give you peace of mind and will make your heart glad."[3]

Psalm 127:3-5

"Children are a gift from the Lord; they are a reward from him. Children born to a young man are like arrows in a warrior's hands. How joyful is the man whose quiver is full of them! He will not be put to shame when he confronts his accusers at the city gates."[4]

According to Scripture children are precious and a blessing. As parents we are to teach, train and discipline them. Success isn't even mentioned, which makes me wonder if we are actually called to success and if success is actually part of the parenting equation?

IS THE ONUS ALL ON US?

As parents we often feel the onus is squarely on us to produce kids who turn out right. Kids who grow up to be church-going, God-fearing adults. There is a lot of Christian literature that will support this—if we do a, b and c it will equal d. I am not sure that is accurate. As far as I understand, the onus isn't all on us. It is a three-part equation:

God – He has promised to pursue our kids as He isn't willing for any to perish

Free Choice –We all have the gift of choice, to choose Him or not and our kids have that same choice

Me and My Faithfulness – How I live out my faith before my kids, how I teach, train, discipline and love them

The only part of that equation that I have control over is me. What if God is calling parents to be faithful? I wonder what would happen if we began to measure our parenting by faithfulness instead of success?

FAITHFULNESS

Several years ago I came across one of the best articles I have ever read on the subject of parenting, success and faithfulness.[5] I will share the gist of it with you because it profoundly impacted me and how I parent. The author likens our task of pointing our kids to Jesus to the assignment the prophet Ezekiel was given with the people of Israel.

Ezekiel was an Old Testament prophet, though Scripture doesn't tell us if he was a parent, his assignment to the people of Israel has incredible similarities to parenthood and the matter of success and faithfulness. God appointed Ezekiel to be a prophet and warned him that he was being sent to his own people, a people set in revolt against God. His job was to be God's mouthpiece saying, "this is what the Sovereign Lord says… " God told Ezekiel that the people will not listen to him anymore than they listen to God himself. His job was going to be hard—more difficult than he could ever imagine. The Bible says that Ezekiel left with the Spirit of God upon him, returning to his people and sitting on the banks of the river for seven days, overwhelmed, bitter and angry—so beautifully human!

How successful was Ezekiel? The destruction he foretold played out in every gruesome detail. From our point of view his mission was an utter failure. God instructed Ezekiel to speak His words to Israel "whether they listen or fail to listen" and the third time He added that, "they would know that a prophet of God was amongst them."

Ezekiel's responsibility was to speak and embody God's words in such a way that they would know who God is and that he was a righteous prophet of God. I imagine Ezekiel wanted more than this, and I think he desperately wanted his people to turn back to God and escape judgement and death. Scripture doesn't tell us if any repented as a result of Ezekiel's words. But Ezekiel was never held accountable for the repentance of others, but rather for his steadfast obedience—his *faithfulness*.

Friends, though we desperately want our kids to walk with Jesus and give their lives to Him, we are not responsible for their response. We are, however, responsible for how we faithfully live out our faith before them—how we point our kids to Jesus. We need to speak and embody God's words in such a way that our kids will know who God is and that a righteous prophet of God is with them—you!

We are but a third of the equation and the only piece we have control over is our part—our faithfulness. We have the privilege of living out our faith daily before our kids, in the boring, everyday mundane things. Our kids are watching us, they watch how we respond under stress, how we react when hard times hit and how we celebrate when things go well. They are observing what we make a priority, what we make time for and the value we place on things. They see how our time is spent—we get to model our relationship with Christ in front of them. So this begs the question, what are we modelling?

Unknowingly, I was modelling to my kids the need to get ahead financially. They saw that my worth was based on what I could do and how much I could balance on an overflowing plate. I was showing them that my identity and value was in what I could do, not in who I was. How was I to model who God is when I had so little time to spend with Him? How was I to point them to Him, if we were running from event to event and experience to experience?

The obstacle of success that entangled me was like looking into the mirror with my eyes closed. I couldn't see what it actually reflected, I only saw what I wanted to see—an illusion that we were thriving and flourishing as a family—a fantasy. I was confronted with the truth of the reflection when the illusion began to shatter and my understanding of success was unveiled. We weren't thriving as a family, but were instead barely surviving and that was the true reflection of the mirror. Before I could continue on this journey of learning how to pass my faith on to my kids, I had to look at the illusion I was living—the illusion I was perpetuating. I had to see it for what it really was. I needed to acknowledge where we were as a family before we could move forward and make a change. The gift of this hurdle was the undoing and redefining of success. It was embracing the truth of where our family was at, and the call of faithfulness that God was inviting us to. Freedom was unfolding as I examined and unpacked each obstacle the Lord placed on my path. He continued to give *the gift of freedom,* each time I stopped to lean in.

EMBRACING THE GIFT

A Moment to Reflect

- How are you feeling after reading this chapter?
- What is on your plate?
- Is there anything you need to let go of or remove from your plate?
- How are you measuring your parenting?
- What is the atmosphere or tone like in your family?
- What do you want the atmosphere to be like in your family?
- Is there anything you could do differently?
- What is one thing you could do this week to begin to cultivate the atmosphere you desire?

Part 2

THE GIFT UNWRAPPED...

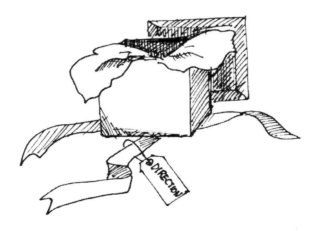

There was a new energy and excitement in my step after working through the obstacles that entangled me. The blinders were off and I could see what entraps me. I was walking in *the gift of freedom* that was given to me in the first part of the journey and things were good!

But before I could run full steam ahead, I was confronted by something else...not so much an obstacle, but more of an embracing or acceptance of my own reality. My eyes were so focused on the goal of figuring out the *practicals* of passing faith on, that I was blinded to the current state of what was right in front of me. Excited to chart a course, I found myself stuck...not knowing exactly where I was or how to proceed ahead.

I found myself eager to continue on and yet restless because I didn't know where to begin. What a delight to discover that this next leg of the journey would be about unwrapping *the gift of direction*.

Chapter 5

Where Am I and Where Do I Want to Be?

Pink and yellow balloons flanked the floral "Happy Birthday" banner fastened to the wall. Multicoloured ribbons dangling from balloons gently danced in the breeze of the warm fall morning. The aroma of fresh-baked cupcakes still lingered in the kitchen as the kids and I set the table. A bright new tablecloth, scattered with decorative ladybugs and bees, brought the table to life. Bowls of candy and chocolate lined the table along with vibrant bags of icing and sprinkles. Cupcakes sat on their stand like royalty on thrones, waiting to be adorned by eight unsuspecting nine-year-olds as soon as they arrived. The anticipation was mounting and it took my debate team skills to persuade the kids to wait until our guests arrived.

The sun was bursting through the glass front door warming up the foyer as I caught my breath on the stairs. It was unusual to have a few moments to ponder before the hopes of the day materialized. Giggles arose from the basement and the sounds of marbles zooming down their track descended from the older kids playing upstairs. I was jerked out of my dreamy calm by sobering thoughts that pierced deeply: "My baby is turning nine today... in nine more years she will be 18. She could move out and go to college at that point. She has potentially spent half her life with us and I may only have half left. I spent the first half of her life pregnant and nursing... simply surviving. If I only have nine more years left, I have some decisions to make about how I want to spend them!"

It was an abrupt awakening, being yanked out of Never Never Land. Coming to terms with this reality left me feeling panicky and regretful for missed opportunities and possibilities. I began to wonder about what might have been squandered during this nine-year period that evaporated like a warm summer shower on hot pavement. People weren't kidding when they said *the days are long but the years are short*. It is at times like this that my "cup half empty" self criticizes and throws fear around like confetti, while the "cup half full" self wraps me in a soft, heated blanket, graciously calming and soothing me, reminding me of the good times and all the changes and challenges that marked that season. However, it was time to take a closer look.

STATISTICS

As I was researching how to live out my faith before my kids I came across some fascinating statistics. One study[1] reported that firstborns had the highest probability of walking with their faith into adulthood and that it significantly lessened with each child that followed. Another survey concluded that "90% of kids active in high school youth groups do not go to church by the time they are sophomores in college. One third will never return."[2] Not so encouraging for this mom of four. These statistics frustrated me.

The enemy seems to be subtly picking off our kids one at a time over the span of 18 years. Do we not see the red flashing lights, warning us of imminent danger? Why are we not addressing this and giving it the priority it demands? If we were told that if we sent our kids to school tomorrow only 60% would come home, wouldn't we all be homeschooling? Yet when we are confronted with statistics like these, our response seems so passive—is it because it happens slowly and subtly over two decades? I will not stand for these statistics to be true for my family or for yours!

A group of kids in Grades 7 to 12 were polled in another study[3] that asked about who had the most significant spiritual influence in their lives. I felt confident that my impact would be substantial when my kids were little, but I assumed it would wane as they got older and the influence of friends and media would grow. This study showed that my influence was incredibly valuable and wanted, even when I thought it was dissipating. Across the board in each grade, mom and dad ranked in the top two spots, as the most significant spiritual influence during that time period. In his book *Transforming Children into Spiritual Champions*, George Barna highlighted this research: "We discovered that in a typical week, fewer than 10% of parents who regularly attend church with their kids read the Bible together, pray together (other than at meal times) or participate in an act of service as a family unit."[4]

It seems that the lack of faith lived out in ordinary daily routine, and the inadequacy of how we speak about faith in the home tragically impacts our kids and their faith journey. I wonder if parents like myself take for granted the impact we have as our kids get older and unknowingly abdicate it to others. I am curious if others find themselves lulled in the day-to-day of living and forget to plan the years with purpose. If nothing else, these statistics let us know that the odds are not in our favour as it pertains to our kids adopting our faith and walking with the Lord. The chance is even slimmer if we don't do it purposefully.

SURVEY THE LAND

Dr. Phil is famous for his simple, profound saying: "You can't change what you don't acknowledge."[5] I had to accept where I was at, before I could do anything differently. I needed to take a hard, honest look at where our family was and review our situation. Coming to terms with the fact that we had spent much of our time living in survival mode wasn't easy. Each time a family goes through a significant change, it takes a while to find equilibrium again. It might be a new baby, a job change or moving to a new place. We find ourselves in this place of "surviving" or "just getting through" until we discover our balance and get our footing again. Every family goes through this phase, often multiple times—it's normal. However, I forgot to leave it. It was supposed to be a temporary resting spot, a place to catch your breath—not a place to settle and put down roots.

I had gotten so bogged down in the daily grind that I forgot to dream the big picture stuff for my family. What do I want to impart to my kids and how am I going to do it? What character qualities do I want to purposefully cultivate in them? What kind of adults do I want these kids to become? It was time to dream and plan. Time to go before the Lord and seek Him in prayer—time to listen for the future He has designed for our family.

"The first step towards getting somewhere is to decide that you are not going to stay where you are."[6] I was not content to stay in survival mode anymore. It had served its purpose but we'd probably overstayed our welcome. It was time to move on.

THE TYRANNY OF THE URGENT

I spent many days feeling like a raft in the water being tossed about during a howling storm. I had dreams and plans, but I couldn't seem to bring them into fruition. I was often reacting to whatever or whoever demanded the most attention.

The first area we chose to be intentional about was spending more one-on-one time with each of our kids. Though we wanted to spend quality time with our kids, it always seemed to be interrupted by the tyranny of the urgent. Our goal wasn't lofty— we aimed for one parent to spend two hours of one-on-one time with each child a month. After a full year of trying to implement this, we were dumbfounded at how often something else came up and hijacked our time.

I sat at our kitchen table which was camouflaged by the remnants of breakfast, a toddler on my knee, and the enchanted aroma of coffee brewing. I took the calendar down from the fridge and began to look at our commitments for the month. I was struck at our ability to honour all our doctors' appointments. If we can make it to the doctor, why can't we make the one-on-one dates happen for the kids? Savouring a reassuring cup of comfort, I remembered a saying I once heard: "A dream is just a dream until it's written down, then it becomes a goal."[7] If I want one-on-one time to happen, I have to treat it like a doctor's appointment and purposefully schedule it in the calendar. From that moment on, every Tuesday night became kids' date night, which we have continued to honour even now that our kids are 18, 16, 14 and 12. A dream can materialize into a goal, and then reality. Honouring your dream involves guarding that time and making it a priority. The tyranny of the urgent will always try to usurp and deflate dreams before they can unfold into existence.

CALENDAR

Several years ago I was challenged to use my calendar as a mirror and see what it reflects back. I picked up our colourful calendar of a month ago along with a fresh new blank one and began to analyze where and how our time was spent. Just like we have fixed and variable expenses, we also have fixed and variable time. Certain commitments on our calendar can't be moved. We have to honour things like work and school. However we do have some flexibility in how we spend our variable time. I felt tired as I looked at our colour-coded calendar. It was crowded and had very little white space. It felt cluttered, which made me feel scattered. On one hand I took pride in what we could accomplish, and on the other hand I felt overwhelmed. I love people and I love down time. I began to ponder what I wanted my month to look like. If I had three goals that month, what would they be? What was really important to me? Was it reflected in my over-crowded, chock-full, colour-coded calendar? I felt like my calendar was in charge of me, telling me where to go and what to do. I forgot that I was the one colouring, highlighting and arranging all these events and then somehow missing the things that really mattered most to me.

Ask your kids what they think you spend most of your time doing.

It may not be accurate or true, but it is the truth from their point of view. My kids thought I spent all of my time in the kitchen, doing laundry or in front of the computer. Not necessarily correct, but that is how they saw it. Granted, I was in the kitchen a lot and laundry was a dragon I could never seem to slay. I changed a few things after hearing that, like deciding not to open the laptop when the kids were around. I didn't want to be distracted by lesser things when they were present. I wanted them to know that I prefer them over the computer and that I value relationships over screens. Taking our kids' perspective into account can help us communicate love and value to them. It helps us to speak their language in a way that makes them feel cherished and significant.

Sometimes we need a jolt out of our slumber—I know I sure did. I got so busy in the day to day of life that I forgot to plan for the bigger picture. In the midst of nourishing, playing, cleaning and loving, I forgot to dream and plan for the adults I wanted my kids to become. In searching how to practically point my kids to Jesus, the first leg of the journey was marked by freedom, with the undoing of obstacles that entangled me. This new leg seemed to be marked by an awakening to living life purposefully—discovering *the gift of direction*.

EMBRACING THE GIFT

A Moment to Reflect

- What are you feeling after reading this?
- Are you in a season of survival?
- How will you know when it is time to move on?
- What are your hopes and dreams for your family?
- What do you want to cultivate in your home and in your kids?
- How can you begin to implement your dreams?
- Write down some next steps.

Chapter 6

Charting the Course

Aware of the obstacles that entrapped me, I traded in the overstuffed, cumbersome backpacks for new-found freedom. I felt lighter; joy became my companion and expectation blew in. I was finally starting to make some headway in this journey of making an invisible faith visible. With eyes wide open, I could honestly see where our family was. I knew what was going well and where we could do things differently. With cloudy glasses wiped clean, clarity, vision and direction dialled into focus. Excitement to move forward was surging and the anticipation was unmistakable. Aware of how our time was being managed and all that foraged for it was liberating. By purposely leaving survival mode, we entered into a whole new world of dreaming and planning. I felt like a racehorse locked in my gate, impatiently waiting for the doors to open. Faithfully pointing my kids to Jesus was my goal. Living my life in such a way that they would know who God is was my target. I couldn't wait to start… and then it all came to a screeching halt. How the heck do I do this? Where in the world do I begin?

I love making order out of chaos. Give me an overflowing, cluttered, disorganized closet and I revel in sorting through it all. Creating piles of valuables to keep, eliminating the excess and collecting the "usables" to give to someone else, brings me a sense of joy and accomplishment. Whether it is a junk drawer, a garage or a room, finding a home for everything is gratifying. Starting in one corner, I sort and discard my way clear across the room, leaving order and tidiness in my wake. I love simplifying and keeping only what is necessary. There is such freedom in letting go of the stuff that weighs us down.

Physical space is often a good reflection of our head space. I enjoy coming alongside others and helping them in this process. You can see the external physical transformation seep into their mind and emotions, and internally order rolls in and peace begins to settle. Not knowing where to start is the biggest obstacle for those who feel overwhelmed by the decluttering process.

I know where to begin and how to navigate organizing a room, but knowing where to start as it pertained to passing faith on to my kids stumped me. I needed someone to point me in the right direction. Like a ship docked in harbour, I knew where I was, I knew where I wanted to go, but I needed someone to show me how to chart the course.

Around that time, I attended a family ministry conference where Mark Holmen was the main speaker. What he said resonated deeply within me. For the first time someone put words to the groaning of my heart. Needless to say I ordered all three of his books and anxiously awaited their arrival. As I dove into the first book, I responded with an audible "aha" by the first few pages. Not only did he articulate my same concerns about passing faith on, but he tangibly outlined where to begin. In his book, *Faith Begins at Home*, he outlined three specific starting points.[1]

MAKE A COMMITMENT

It may seem simple and rather insignificant, but there is something to be said about making a decision. On our wedding day, I made a commitment to James and he to me. We chose each other and we promised not to look elsewhere. We vowed from that day on that we would be faithful to each other. We pledged to love when it's easy and when it's difficult. We made that commitment, through vows, in front of our family and friends. They bore witness to our covenant.

In Joshua 24:13-27, Moses challenges the Israelites as they are crossing into the promised land. He reminds them of God's faithfulness to them and His provision. He charges them to align themselves with the Living God anew and to place their allegiance to Him alone. They responded with a vow to serve Him and obey His commands wholeheartedly. Joshua responds by taking a large stone and placing it under an oak tree;

> " 'See!' he said to all the people. 'This stone will be a witness against us. It has heard all the words the Lord has said to us. It will be a witness against you if you are untrue to your God.' " Joshua 24:27[2]

Sometimes we need a tangible reminder of the things we have chosen to commit ourselves to. This is the value of celebrating anniversaries, it is a hands-on way of remembering a promise and why it was made. Take a wedding band—it is a visual representation of a vow made with another person. It is a symbol of a promise and a commitment.

Each family must choose for themselves to make a commitment

to serve the Lord and obey His commands. Just as the Israelites chose to realign themselves and pledge their allegiance anew to the Living God, so must we. Find a symbol, something that is a tangible reminder of your promise so that you are reminded of it each time you see it. It could be a rock or something in nature, a Scripture verse, or a family mission statement—anything that is a visible representation of an invisible commitment.

PRAY THROUGH YOUR HOME

Home is a gift. Whether we own it or rent it, it becomes an extension of us. It is where we are most authentically ourselves. A place of rest, refuge and safety. A spot where love becomes tangible and acceptance secured… at least we hope it is.

Taking ownership of a new space is exciting, but sometimes things are left behind by the previous owners—garbage, old furniture, even their dirt. Before we move all of our belongings in, we clean the house from top to bottom, discarding anything left behind.

Immaterial things can be left behind too. We don't know the spiritual baggage of the old owners or what they have allowed to transpire in the home. Violence or trauma are too often found within the family home. It isn't uncommon today to find those involved in the occult or others who have shrines set up to other gods. As believers, it is critical that we dedicate not only ourselves, but all that we are and all that we have to the Lord—especially our living space.

This is something James and I have chosen to do every year on the first day of school. We pray through each room of our home and our property, out loud and anoint it with oil. We anoint it with oil because in Biblical times oil was a symbol of the presence of the Holy Spirit. It was common-place in Scripture, for both people and items to be anointed with oil for the sole purpose of consecrating and setting them apart for the Lord.

Because I like to have something to follow, we pray a prayer like this one, which is written by my dear friend Beth Graf. You are welcome to use it, or use it as a jumping-off point to make it your own.

I declare afresh that I (we), (full name and any other family members) belong to the True Lord Jesus Christ of Nazareth as well as all that I am (we are) and have and every aspect of my (our) life. I submit the whole of my (our) life into the Loving Hands of the Holy Father, the Holy Son and the Holy Spirit. I surrender myself (us) completely to the Lordship of the True Lord Jesus Christ of Nazareth now.

In the strong name of the Lord Jesus Christ of Nazareth and as the rightful owner/tenant of this home and property, I, (full name of owner/s), declare that every square inch of my (our) home and property belongs to the Lord Jesus Christ of Nazareth and only HIM.

The cross and blood of the Lord Jesus Christ of Nazareth overrides all that has occurred either on the land of this home or anything that has happened within or around this home now, in the name of the Lord Jesus Christ of Nazareth.

All curses, all words spoken and actions that are not of You Lord Jesus, against me and my family or this home and property are made null and void, in the name of the Lord

Jesus Christ of Nazareth now!

I ask You, Holy Spirit, to blaze through this home and property and remove all that is not of You, every thing and every being. Please replace it with all that is of You, Holy Spirit.

Lord Jesus Christ of Nazareth, as I go around my home and property now, I ask that You would force the kingdom of darkness in its entirety to adhere to the sign of Your Holy Cross.

Please Holy Spirit help me (us) and lead me (us) as I (we) reclaim my (our) home and property for the Lord Jesus Christ of Nazareth.

I pray all these things in the name of the Holy Father, the Holy Son and the Holy Spirit, Amen.

We pray this prayer out loud because it declares to the kingdom of darkness that this space and all who live in it are consecrated to God. Initially, anointing and praying through your home is like establishing spiritual walls and boundaries around your living space. Doing it annually is a good maintenance practice and a reminder of our commitment. It points out the atmosphere we desire for our guests to experience when they enter our home.

To anoint your home, you need some oil that you have committed to the Lord, dab it on your finger and mark the cross at the entrance points of your home and your property lines. We pray out loud because the enemy can't read our thoughts, but they can hear what we say audibly. Commit each room to the Lord and ask the

Holy Spirit to remove all that is not of Him and replace it with His Holy presence. My friend Beth teaches a great truth: "Authority over powers of darkness is entry-level Christianity—as soon as you receive Christ—you've got it. His authority isn't something we earn, it is bestowed to us."

FAMILY MISSION STATEMENT

There is a reason large corporations and businesses have a mission statement. It keeps them on track and focused on what their target is. It keeps them from getting distracted or wasting time and resources on things that may be valuable, but not necessarily what they have been tasked to do.

It is so easy for us to get swallowed up by all the good things that are calling our name. There are hundreds of good opportunities your family can get involved in, but you only have so much variable time. The truth is, you only have room for the great things. So how do we determine what the great things for our family are? How do we sift out the great from the good? This is the purpose of a family mission statement.

Several years ago James and I embarked on this task. It was challenging. We researched family mission statements and how to create them. It forced us to examine what we really value as a family. It made us look at our absolutes. We were compelled to reflect on what we want our family to be known for. It was a great exercise. We had to articulate our values. Reflecting on what I want others to say about my family was a profound jumping-off point for me. We slowly began to draft out our hopes and dreams, our commitments and our covenants. Our goal was to keep it simple, so that our young kids would understand it.

This is what we came up with:

The Cabral Family…
- *Loves Jesus*
- *Will be real about our faith and live it out in truth*
- *Wants to love unconditionally, encourage, nurture and forgive one another*
- *Wants to honour God in our family, our friendships, our church and in our community*
- *Wants to share our home, our things, our money and our time*
- *Wants our invisible faith to be visible through our words, actions and attitudes*

Many families include their kids in this process. Ours were pretty little at the time, so James and I decided to set the tone for our family. It has been said *if we don't know what we stand for, we fall for anything*. If we don't know what our values are, we get involved in and distracted by all the good things and we miss out on the great ones!

The *great* will be different for each family as our unique combination of values, spiritual gifts and passions are different. We turned down a fantastic mid-week, faith-based program for our kids because it was more valuable to us to make one-on-one time with them a priority during that time slot. Not all would agree with us, but turning down a good opportunity, made room for great heartfelt conversations between our kids and us as parents. What a privilege to uncover what your *great* is! The value of a family mission statement is that you can weigh each good opportunity against your mission statement. It becomes a tool to help you sift and sort through all the good things alluring you. It will aid you in keeping focused and staying on the unique course designed for your family.

THREE ESSENTIALS

In the process of figuring out where to start, a few other "must-have" essentials rose to the surface. They would become quintessential in gaining momentum and sustaining the journey we were on.

Putting Family First

We had to make our nuclear family our number one priority. Yes, our relationship with God and nurturing and growing that was first, nourishing our marriage and making room for each other, second—but making family the priority was essential. As a recovering people-pleaser, I find it hard to say no. My mind naturally responds "yes" initially and then often feels regret. I have had to learn to respond with "let me think about that" before committing to anything. That little bit of time gives me a chance to pray about it, chat it over with James and weigh it against our family mission statement before agreeing to anything. I spent years frustrated for taking on things that I didn't really want to do. My family paid the price for my choices when I said "yes" before taking a moment to pray. Though I said they were what was most important to me—my first priority—they would get the tired, burnt out, nothing-left-to-give mom/wife who had said "yes" to too many things. Those I couldn't say no to got the upbeat, oh-so-helpful, delightful me.

Living Counter-cultural

We knew that we were going to live counter-culturally—that decision seemed logical and it is actually what our faith calls us to do in many aspects of our life. Sometimes, however, it was hard watching that play out. We chose to limit our kids' extracurricular activities for two reasons. One was financial—we chose to live on a single income and there was only so much disposable money available. The other was probably more important to us as a family, and it was that I didn't want to be driving and schlepping kids from activity to activity and game to game. That wasn't how we wanted to spend our variable time. I knew many families who thrived on this, but I knew it wasn't the best choice for our family. By nature, my kids are introverts. They love people and adore time spent with others, but it tires them out. Dragging them from place to place wasn't going to go well. I knew I would be rushing them out the door and that they wouldn't necessarily want to go. Though this was the best decision, there was fallout. Because my kids weren't involved in organized sports, their peers were much more skilled. When it came to trying out for school sports, they were often cut as they didn't have the level of skill of those practised peers. There are consequences for our choices, even the ones we know are the best for our family. Coming to terms with them is part of the journey.

What caught me by surprise was when I realized that we were going to have to live counter to church culture too. I love the local church and church community is something I encourage and deeply value. Church, like other organizations, can be activity-driven as well. They have incredible events and opportunities to get involved in. What we quickly realized was that though they are good and edifying, we could spend all of our variable time there. If we attended all the children, youth, men, women and family opportunities, we would have no family time left. We had to weigh these good opportunities against our mission statement and make *best* choices based on that.

Choosing Simplicity

If our most important goal is to faithfully point our kids to Jesus it was going to require a life marked by simplicity and large margins for our family. These things, the *greater* things, require time and unhurried moments—at least for our family they do. As school and work account for the majority of our time, we have purposefully kept our evenings and weekends light. The freedom to linger is a gift I want my kids to know. The choice to have home days where we can lounge in our pyjamas, play games or binge watch Netflix is time I want them to appreciate. They value choice and having a voice in how that down time is spent, and I want to honour that. So much of life is hurrying from event to event, grabbing things on the fly and rushing. I wanted our family to be marked by the polar opposite of busyness. I wanted it to be marked by the opportunity to savour, rest and lag in the moment. Choosing simplicity is a tough balance between managing the expectations of others and guarding our family time, and we are still working out that balance.

Discovering where to start was instrumental in moving forward on this journey. Uncovering the essential must-haves for this adventure set us up to chart a course that would gain momentum and sustain longevity. Like manna falling from Heaven for the Israelites in the wilderness, so the Lord faithfully provided for this leg of the journey too, sprinkling people and resources across our path. As we pressed on and moved forward, we continued to unwrap *the gift of direction* He laid out for us.

EMBRACING THE GIFT

A Moment to Reflect

- What is stirring within you after reading this?
- Is there anything you need to invite Jesus to speak into?
- Is there a commitment you need to make?
- What is a tangible symbol that can remind you of your commitment?
- What are your thoughts around praying through your home?
- Spend some time sifting through your values and what's important to you.
- Begin to create your family mission statement.

Free Gift: Creating a Family Mission Statement.
Go to: leannecabral.com/book-resources

Part 3

THE GIFT IN ACTION...

Intentionality

The summit was now with in sight… the information I was so desperately seeking was coming into focus. Everything that I initially believed to be the sole purpose of this adventure was at my fingertips. It amazes me that we think we know what we are looking for only to discover that the Lord shows us exactly what we really need. The first leg of the journey was about my own untangling and *the gift of freedom* I was given. The next leg was about taking stock of my surroundings; having the truth of my reality mirrored back to me by the One who only speaks Truth. As I unwrapped that gift, *direction* emerged.

Now embarking on the third leg of this quest, expectancy billowed. This journey has been rich. Roots have had time to burrow a little deeper. Dry rot and dead branches have been pruned away making room for new life. There was a settledness… an assurance that the One who tends to the roots is in control. My anticipation of impending knowledge and understanding for the practical on-the-ground application was unmistakable. I could see the destination!

Be careful though, dear reader, not to get tripped up in this leg of the journey by feeling overwhelmed by all the possibilities and options. Do not let discouragement creep in. This story comes to you from the context of my story of a nuclear family.

Though I initiated the majority of this, I had a husband who was supportive and on board. Your situation may be different. You may be parenting on your own. Maybe your spouse hasn't met Jesus yet. Do not lose hope because you can use these same tools and adjust them to meet your unique needs and circumstances. The Lord is Faithful. He will be a Father to the Fatherless , (or Mother to the Motherless) and a defender of widows (Psalm 68:5). Trust the Lord to lead and guide you. If fear starts to nip at your heels, look up at the One who sees the entire path and trust Him to calm your mind, soothe your soul and direct your steps, because now you get to see *the gift in action!*

Chapter 7

Prayer

Eagerly anticipating dinner, four children aged six and under sat around our kitchen table. Brightly coloured placemats hosted standard issue Ikea plastic tableware. Pouring milk into her siblings' cups, the six-year-old outlined why four-and two-year-olds couldn't be trusted with this task. They held their own as they tried to convince her that they were quite capable and they should have a turn. With a green bean squished in each hand the baby smiled and watched the exchange between his sisters and brother. Preferences were clearly expressed as dinner was dished out onto their plates. James and I sat down as we all joined hands and thanked the Lord for our dinner.

Our mealtimes were often chaotic. Drinks rarely stayed upright and food seemed to prefer residence on the floor instead of on our plates or in our bellies. Someone usually ended up crying over something, while others couldn't seem to keep their hands to themselves. Giving instructions, managing behaviour and mopping up spilled milk seemed to monopolize most of our time, energy and conversation. At the end of one rather ridiculous mealtime I looked at James and said: "Do you think will we ever have a nice meal with real conversation?"

Meals times are tricky when kids are little and clearly outnumber you—there is a lot going on! By routine my kids knew to fold their hands, close their eyes and say grace before they ate, but anything more than that quickly became a gong show. I longed to figure out how to teach them about prayer and incorporate different kinds of prayer activities. Each time we tried to pray with them outside of meals and bed times, I felt like I was refereeing a wrestling match, herding cats or wrangling cattle.

I knew the value of prayer, the significance of an ongoing conversation with our Creator. I understood that prayer fosters and cultivates our relationship with God and creates a space to listen and respond. I appreciated that prayer needed to be modelled as well as taught and I wanted to figure out how to teach my kids to pray. I knew there was so much more to prayer than simply "fold your hands and close your eyes." While my kids may have mastered their prayer manners, I wanted them to learn how to converse with their Creator. I had a sneaking suspicion that it probably wasn't as complicated as it seemed. I longed to know these methods that I hadn't yet discovered—the tools of the trade that teach kids how to pray.

As parents we often long for our kids to be better than us. To make better choices than we did. We hope that they can avoid some of the mistakes we made. However when it comes to prayer, how will they learn beyond what they see? If we want our kids to become great prayers, we are going to have to become great prayers ourselves. They mimic what they see and this conversation about prayer begins with us—the parents.

OBSTACLES

I think there are many reasons why it can be difficult for adults to pray. Praying out loud can be intimidating. We can become self-conscious and insecure about our thoughts, the words we choose and how it sounds. Yet Matthew 6:7-8 says:

> *"And when you pray, do not keep on babbling like pagans, for they think they will be heard because of their many words. Do not be like them, for your Father knows what you need before you ask him."[1]*

For others, prayer might be hard simply because it isn't a routine yet. It has been said that it only takes six weeks to make a habit stick. Choosing natural rhythms in the day is a great way to start to create a routine. In the car, on the way to work, or as you shower in the morning are great daily opportunities to pray.

Sometimes I wonder if we doubt the effectiveness of our prayers. If God is sovereign and fully accomplishes His purposes, does it really matter if I pray? Will it make a difference? The Bible clearly shows God's desire to hear our requests and that He listens when we call out to Him. Abraham pleaded with God about Sodom and Gomorrah; God responded and the criteria was altered. In Revelation, John talks about the significance of our prayers when he refers to the "prayer bowls of the saints." In Luke 18:1-8, Jesus tells a parable of the persistent widow. As she relentlessly brings her plea before the ungodly judge who finally concedes to her requests, how much more will "God bring about justice for his chosen ones, who cry out to him day and night? Will he keep putting them off?"[2]

Early on, wanting to pray like someone else was an obstacle for me. I had a dear friend who prayed so beautifully and eloquently. The words she chose, the cadence of her voice, even the things she thought to pray about were inspiring to me—I desperately wanted to pray like her. We are all one-of-a-kind creations—there are no duplicates. His desire is for us is to be authentic and pray true to how He has designed us. Learning to embrace my own unique prayer personality was vital. I may not be an eloquent prayer, but I have learned to accept the way He has created me. My prayers may start suddenly and end abruptly—they may sound more like a machine gun as they come fast and furious and unexpectedly stop, but that is how I am uniquely made.

PRAYING FOR OUR KIDS

I was curious as to what other parents were praying for their kids. I only knew to pray about the things that crossed my mind. The themes of my prayers were about salvation, protection and wisdom. I prayed for their future spouses and the families that were raising them, hoping that those families might be praying for us and our children too. Praying that my kids would learn to hear God's voice and respond in obedience was important to me. Asking the Holy Spirit to affirm them when they make right choices and make them feel unsettled when they were making poor choices was a common prayer as well.

In this season where I was researching all that I could about kids, families and prayer, a friend came over for coffee one morning. She and her husband had just adopted a beautiful baby girl. Excitement and joy flowed from her as she cradled this beautiful bundle of hope and possibilities in her arms. I asked her what she prayed for her daughter. She look a little perplexed and then matter of factly replied, "I just ask the Lord what to pray for her and pray that." My jaw dropped—that is something I never considered. How brilliant! Of course seeking the Creator about His created is common sense—He would know her intimately, as He designed her. He knows what her struggles will be, where the enemy will try to gain ground. He knows how she is uniquely wired and exactly what she requires intercession for. So simple, so wise, so obvious, and yet it never even crossed my mind.

Around that same time, I met another friend one afternoon and I asked her the same question. She hesitantly responded that what she was about to say was going to sound a little off-the-wall and to let her explain. My curiosity was piqued and I was intrigued. She went on to say that she asked the Lord for a symbol in nature for each of her kids. She wanted a symbol that would remind her children of who they were and how God saw them. She wanted this symbol to call out to her kids, especially if they went through a season of not walking with Him. It would serve as a reminder of who they are and God's incredible affection for them. Genius, right?!? That night James and I prayed a similar prayer for our kids and He lovingly brought an image in nature to mind for each of them along with specific words of identity and purpose for them. For Seth, our youngest, He gave us the image of waves: *"Seth, you are like the waves. You are healing water. You will wash over people and knock them off their feet. You will bring comfort, laughter and healing to the broken."*

We live right by Lake Ontario and each time Seth walks by the lake he is reminded of who he is and how God sees him. Really, it is no different than Peter in the Bible. He too had a symbol. Each time he saw a rooster he was reminded of God's incredible love and forgiveness for him. Perhaps this is something that might be of value to your family too.

TEACHING OUR KIDS TO PRAY

"Praying for our kids is important and it impacts now and eternity, praying with our kids teaches them to become prayers themselves and hear the voice of God."[3]

Why are our kids' prayers so significant? I came across a great book by Cheryl Fuller and she beautifully outlined the value of our kids' prayers in her book, *When Children Pray*. Here are some of her thoughts intertwined with my own.

Kids who have invited Jesus to be their forever friend are a significant part of the Body of Christ. They possess unique qualities that make them significant prayer warriors. Their faith is an *"all things are possible"* kind of faith. They haven't learned the caution and cynicism that often comes with adulthood. Most kids naturally possess big faith. I wonder if *their wide-eyed wonder, openness and expectation that Jesus found so endearing and may have prompted Him to say that we all should approach His Throne with these childlike qualities.* I wonder if their prayers are so effective because their tenderheartedness reflects the heart of Jesus. There is no miniature version of the Holy Spirit. The same Holy Spirt that indwells you and I fully lives in our children who have chosen Him. Oh, the power we are missing by not including our kids in our adult prayer gatherings—we are omitting half the Body! Kids are able to pray big prayers and release them to God in ways that are different and hard for us to do as adults. Perhaps we need to trust God a little more and allow our kids to pray for the difficult and complicated situations.[4]

Several years ago I was stunned to find out I was pregnant with our fifth baby. We prayed for and planned each one of our kids and this unanticipated gift was a surprise to all of us. After the initial shock wore off, we were beyond thrilled as we planned for this new little one. My first trimester is normally marked by extreme morning/all-day sickness. I take medication to keep food down and avoid hospitalization. We decided to share our news with our then nine, seven, five and three-year-old children pretty early on, as we wanted this little miracle to be celebrated with them and explain why I was so sick. Cheers, clapping and dancing erupted as our elated kids jumped up and down, celebrating great news!

A few days later I began spotting. I had never miscarried before—the thought actually never really crossed my mind. The next two weeks were spent in and out of hospital trying to figure out what was going on. In the midst of that I felt the Lord prompting me to invite our kids into this crisis, letting them pray over this baby and lay hands on him or her. My heart ached. I knew that my faith could withstand a miscarriage, but I wasn't convinced theirs could. I knew that if they prayed for this baby, they would expect a live birth in a few months. Their faith was so new, so fragile—how could they possibly process all of this? As I expressed my concern to the Lord, He clearly spoke: "Leanne as much as you love your kids and are concerned about their spiritual well-being, know that I am more—trust Me with their hearts… with their faith. Trust Me to care for them and to sustain them."

That night they placed their little hands on my belly. Four heartfelt, sincere voices interceded for their sibling. A few days later we found out that the pregnancy was no longer viable as they couldn't find a heartbeat. Though I thought my kids' faith would be forever crushed, it wasn't. Hannah came upstairs, put her head on my shoulder and wept for the sibling she so desperately wanted to meet. Caleb gave me a huge lingering hug, asking me if I was going to be okay. Five-year-old Ella threw herself on my bed sobbing "But I really wanted a baby!!" And Seth who was a little oblivious to all that was happening crawled onto my bed, put his little hands on my cheeks, pulled me right up to his face, saying, "I wuf you mama." We talked about how this baby was in Heaven with Jesus and that one day we will get to meet him or her.

Sometimes we try to protect our kids from praying about the complicated things in life. Fear overtakes our trust in His care for those we hold closest to us. I was dumbfounded at their capacity to roll with all that transpired over a matter of days. It didn't crush their faith—it transformed ours. Trust the One who truly loves them more, and allow Him to grow and nurture their faith especially in difficult, complex situations.

WHERE TO BEGIN...

I think that there are three approaches to cultivating prayer in our home and teaching our kids how to pray: we can establish a routine of prayer time, look for spontaneous opportunities to pray as they pop up, and model a life of prayer in our family.

Routine
Finding consistent times in the rhythm of the day to pray are

great habit-forming opportunities. Kids thrive in routine and we want prayer to become a habit for our kids. Look at your day and see the times that you are all together consistently—those times can be great moments to lead off with prayer or close in prayer. Families often pray before mealtime or bedtime. We pray together as a family each morning on our drive to school. Car rides are a fantastic time to pray—you have a captive audience when everyone is buckled in!

Spontaneous

Ask God for practical, unplanned opportunities to teach your kids to pray. Perhaps seeing or hearing an emergency vehicle can be a reminder to pray for all those involved. Or when the news is on and the kids are within earshot. You can choose to pray when your kids are feeling hurt, sad, scared, happy or about to try something new.

We used a symbol to remind us to pray for a specific person. About eight years ago, family friends found out that their three-year-old daughter had cancer. Our kids were around the same age and we were heartbroken for them as they walked a road no one should have to travel. We wanted to pray regularly for them and so I asked the kids to think about what three-year-old girls love. They all responded with various forms of Disney princesses. So we decided that whenever we saw something Disney or princess-like, that would be our reminder to pray. It was like "eye spy" for them and each time they found our symbol reminder, they responded in prayer.

Around that same time I was asking the Lord to give me practical opportunities to show my kids His presence and provision. Caleb and I were out on a date night at Walmart, he loved wandering the toy aisle. As he pondered and dreamed about all that caught his attention, we walked hand in hand as he shared the value and significance of each one. We knew it was a time to look and explore, not a time for buying more. Walking towards our car, I noticed a man standing by it. Unsettled, I approached our vehicle. The man kindly walked towards me saying, "I noticed you left your lights on and I am parked right in front of you. I thought I'd wait for you in case you needed a boost." Moved by his kindness, I put the key in the ignition, but it wouldn't turn over. He boosted our car for us that evening, allowing us a safe journey home. This was before cell phones were commonplace. I looked over at Caleb and said, "Do you see how God takes care of us? That man chose to wait for us to come out. People don't usually do that, Caleb. Most grown-ups are so busy that they don't have time to wait and help. He may have waited a long time and had he not stayed, we would have been stranded here."

God answers our prayers. He doesn't want to be a mystery to our kids, He wants to reveal Himself to them. My prayer is that we would clearly recognize these moments when they happen.

Role Model
There is such value in letting your kids catch you on your knees. They copy so much of what they see and they will begin to mimic our prayer posture too. You can't change your child's heart and force your kids to follow Jesus—that is God's job and their choice to make.[5] But never underestimate what a powerful role model you can be.

I love sleeping… like, really love it. My kids were forced to become great sleepers because their mom needed a lot of it. I napped every afternoon when my kids went down for a sleep. I napped every day for 11 glorious years and it was awesome! Quiet time with the Lord was sporadic and inconsistent when my kids were little. It was a season where many of us survive on little snacks of truth grabbed between all the other things vying for our attention. During that time I sensed the Lord inviting me to wake up half an hour earlier, while the kids were still sleeping, and spend a few uninterrupted minutes with Him. I reluctantly agreed, but proceeded negotiating the terms: "I will get up half an hour early, but You have to keep the kids sleeping till 7 a.m. I cannot start my day before that." The first morning I got up and tiptoed down stairs at 6:30 a.m, turned on the fireplace, flipped open my journal and Bible and spent some great time in the Word and in prayer. The kiddos woke up at 7 a.m. sharp. The next morning looked very similar except that one child decided to join me at about 6:45. By the end of the week all four kids were up by 6:30 sitting on the sofa with me as I tried to do my devotions. Frustrated, I said to the Lord, "You have got be kidding me—are you serious?!? We had an agreement!" And then this thought crossed my mind: How can I ever expect my kids to spend time with the Lord, in His Word and praying, when they don't see their mom doing it?

PRACTICAL TIPS

Sometimes we all need just a few "how-to" ideas. A common suggestion for prayer is the A.C.T.S. acronym: Adoration, Confession, Thanksgiving and Supplication. These words were too big for our family so we simply taught our kids to pray "thank you", "please" and "I am sorry" prayers. Ask your kids what the best part of their day was and turn it into a thanksgiving prayer.

Ask them good questions that will help them pray. What was the happiest thing that happened today? What was the saddest? Is there anyone you need to forgive? Is there anything you need to ask forgiveness for today? What do you need help with? The answers to these questions are great things to pray about when our kids struggle with what to say.

Allow for silence after each prayer. Part of prayer is listening as well as talking. Teach your kids to ask the Lord if there is anything else He wants to say; and then in silence, listen. We will talk much more about this in Chapter 9.

PRAYER ACTIVITIES

I knew there was more to prayer than "close your eyes and fold your hands." In my quest to find out more I came across some great activities that cultivate prayer in unconventional ways, and keep kids' attention and focus. Let me share a few with you that our kids loved.

Visual Prayers
Prayer Journals – Pencil crayons and journals are a creative form of prayer as our kids can write or draw out their prayers.

Picture Box – Each year at Christmas time we get a lot of family photo Christmas cards. We used to discard them after the season and then feel guilty. One year I decided to keep them and placed them in a Picture Prayer Box to use as a prayer activity. Each person chooses a photo card. We allow a few minutes of silence before we pray so that we can silently ask the Lord what to pray for the family we have chosen. Then we take turns praying out loud for people in the photo cards in front of us. Sometimes a kid would end up praying for the family's cute puppy, but then other times profound, deeper requests were made.

Attribute Box – Praise is a difficult concept for kids to grasp as it describes who God is. It is often mixed up with thanksgiving. We created an Attribute Box filled with cue cards that have one sentence written on them, "I love God because…" Hand them out to your family and let them fill in the blank. Pray them back to God when you're finished.

Jar of Stones – We have a jar of stones that we use as an altar of remembrance for times when the Lord supernaturally stepped in for our family. Sometimes we pick out a stone that has been written on and thank the Lord for His provision. Other times we take a fresh stone and write down a recent time where God showed up so tangibly for us.

Multicoloured Prayer Chain – A family had taken coloured strips of paper and linked them together like a chain. On each link they wrote a specific category to pray about. The seven categories were; Family, Church, Friends, Neighbourhood, School, Missionaries, Government. Each day they chose one category to pray about as a family.

Tactile Prayers
Prayer Structures – This activity doesn't make much sense to adults but it really keeps kids engaged and focused. You can use Play-Do or Lego—anything that can stack or stick together. Hand out three pieces of Lego to each person. During the first round each person picks up one piece of Lego, leaving the other two in front of them. The first person takes their one piece of Lego and passes it to the

person on their left praying, "Thank you God for..." That person attaches the first Lego to theirs and then passes the "structure" to the next person on their left praying "Thank you God for..." They then take the two-piece structure and attach their piece and so on. We typically go three rounds with the second prayer being a "please" prayer and the third one "I am sorry God for..." prayer. At the end you have a crazy prayer structure that has kept kids focused and praying.

Bean Bag Toss – Toss a bean bag back and forth. Each time the bean bag is received the person says a "thank you", "please" or an "I am sorry" prayer. You can do the same activity rolling a ball back and forth, playing basketball or popping bubbles.

Audio Prayers

Whisper Prayers – much like broken telephone, have each member of the family take turns and whisper a prayer in the ear of the person beside them.

Soaking – Sit somewhere comfortable as a family, dim the lights, put on some worship music and allow it to wash over you. Scripture says that God, inhabits the praises of His people (Psalm 22:3). After the music is finished, talk about what came to your mind while you were listening or what you were thinking about. Maybe you saw an image in your mind's eye you could share or a word that you remember from the song.

Dance – My kids loved choreographing dance moves and actions to worship music. It ends up becoming a full body expression of prayer—both fun and profound!

Alphabet Praise[6] – Often in the car my kids loved to do this kind of prayer. We would start "A" and go straight to "Z" saying things we know to be true about God. He is "Awesome", He is "Brave"…

EMBRACING THE GIFT

A Moment to Reflect

- What is stirring within you after reading this chapter?
- Is there anything you need to leave with Jesus?
- What does your prayer life look like—what are you doing well? Is there anything you would like to do differently?
- What do you pray for your kids?
- Ask the Lord what else to pray for your kids.
- What are two things you would like to do to cultivate prayer in your family?

Chapter 8

Blessing

What is a blessing anyway? In trying to understand how to make an invisible faith visible and tangible to my kids, this topic was at the top of my list. Although blessing is mentioned a lot in Scripture and I had a sense that it was significant, I couldn't seem to grasp it. Why else would Esau—a full-grown man, a man's man, a hunter—weep over losing it? In faith circles, the term is used interchangeably with prayer and grace especially in the context of food or a meal. I confused it with birthright too, which had to do with a physical inheritance for first-born children. I had this nagging suspicion that it was something important and that I should lean in to dig a little deeper, even though the true value of it eluded me.

Melissa and Terry Bone, in their book, *The Power of Blessing*, brought a lot of clarity to the issue for me as they beautifully unpacked the significance and relevance of blessing. It was incredibly impactful and life changing in our family as we began to implement what I was learning in this journey. Though I have never met the Bones, I have spent a lot of time in their book. Like good friends who begin to sound alike, I catch myself using their language and a lot of their words because of how it so deeply impacted me. As a result I have unintentionally adopted some of their language. Please know that the majority of what I will share with you in this chapter is their insight—read their book, it will change you!

The Bones broke down blessing into two different categories. They wrote about how when life is pleasing or if we are in good health we call it a "blessing." When we find extra money in an old coat, or when we avoid the traffic ticket we deserve we call it a "blessing." These are material blessings or rewards for obedience.

The blessings that they speak of in their book, the ones I want to explore with you in this chapter are not material blessings or rewards of obedience, but rewards for being born. They are not transactions or something to be earned, but gifts from the Lord. They are not material, but spiritual. They aren't visible or tangible. The "blessing" that I am referring to in this chapter is about depositing spiritual riches and truths in someone's heart.[1]

POWER OF WORDS

According to James 3:1-12 there is tremendous power in our tongue and the words that we speak. God spoke the world into being. By His words things appeared and burst into life. God shared the power of spoken word with us as human beings when He told Adam to name all the animals: "While God's word created everything, Adam's word gave each an identity."[2] To this day our words breathe life or death, and give identity. We can speak words that build others up or ones that tear them down. Like a stone tossed into the water, our words ripple into the spiritual realm too. With them we make pacts, agreements and self-fulfilling prophecies.

Words have the power of impartation; not only do our words

communicate information, they give value.[3] Years ago someone used to say to me, you are just like "so and so." What they meant was that when I said certain things or turned my face a certain way I reminded them of someone. Though this comment came from an innocent place, I didn't receive it that way. As a child I didn't want to be compared to this person. Though they were kind and loving towards me, I thought I was being compared to the negative parts of them. Though it was said as an observation, communicating information—I attached a value to it—a negative one. Words can change the way we think about ourselves. Proverbs 18:21[4] says that the tongue has the power of life and death. According to Terry Bone, "whenever we allow someone with relational influence in our lives to speak words of blessing over us, God works in agreement with those words and makes a spiritual deposit in your soul."[5]

Through words, God puts His name on us.

Numbers 6:22–27

The Lord said to Moses, "Tell Aaron and his sons, 'This is how you are to bless the Israelites. Say to them:
"'"The Lord bless you and keep you;
the Lord make his face shine on you and be gracious to you;
the Lord turn his face toward you and give you peace."'
"So they will put my name on the Israelites, and I will bless them."[6]

I don't fully understand how this works, but if it puts God's name on me—I am in! It reminds me of Woody in the Toy Story movie. Woody had something very special and unique written under his boot: "Andy." It let everyone know who Woody belonged to and he was proud to be owned by Andy. I love having God's name placed on me. I want to be known as His.

"The words we speak are vehicles that transport spiritual blessings from Heaven to Earth. They transform the promises of God from potential in Heaven to power here on Earth."[7] That is where we as parents come into play. Blessing is so significant because we are God's chosen vessels to impart words of blessing to our kids.

WHAT IS A BLESSING?

A blessing is God's favour being poured out in a person's life. Words of blessing impart life and hope, and change the way we think about ourselves. A blessing conveys Heaven's perspective on who we are and where we are meant to go in life[8]—our identity and our purpose. In Hebrew, blessing is the word *barakah* which means "a transmittal of God's favour."[9] To *baruch* is to kneel down by someone, to empower them to prosper and thrive… to do well, to succeed.[10] Blessing refers to the words, deeds and ceremonies that convey Heaven's favour upon our identity and purpose. Words say it. Deeds show it—actions that agree with our words add weight and credibility to what we say. Ceremonies seal it— they validate memorable moments of blessing in our lives with actions that reinforce the sincerity of the words spoken.[11]

Last spring, Hannah, our eldest, graduated from high school. James and I wanted to celebrate the end of one chapter in her life and the beginning of another. We wanted to bless her as she transitioned from high school into university. We invited a group of women to our home one evening. These were women of different ages and stages, who had a significant influence in Hannah's life—

women she loved and respected. As we gathered around food and drink, each woman shared a word of spiritual advice and word of practical advice for Hannah, as she transitioned into this next phase of her life. Their words were wise and helpful—they reminded Hannah of who she is and all that the Lord has called her to. These women affirmed and blessed her with their words, actions and gifts. They prayed for her. They told her where they saw God at work in her life and they pointed out where they saw His character reflected in her. They challenged her and filled her up so that if she might question her worth or direction, she would have a plumb line of truth to keep her grounded.

WHY BLESS OUR KIDS?

Blessing is mentioned more than 300 times in Scripture, so there might be something significant to it. Many times in the Bible, God commands us to bless one another—it is an act of obedience. Jesus was blessed. Not one miracle was performed or one message preached before He received His Father's blessing. As Jesus went to be baptized by John in Mark 1:11 it says, "And a voice came from heaven: 'You are my Son, whom I love; with you I am well pleased.'"[12] Then John, in John 1:29 says, "Look, the Lamb of God, who takes away the sin of the world!"[13] The Father affirmed Jesus' identity and John affirmed His purpose. If the Son of God waited for the Father's blessing before He entered into His earthly ministry, imagine the impact words of blessing could have on our children and the unique calling placed on their lives.

We need to bless our kids because it is a way that we as parents can stand between them and the kingdom of darkness. This world loves to tell our kids of their worth and value, or attempts to convince them of their lack thereof. The prince of this world tries to do that and much more. Do you know how professionals tell the difference between a counterfeit bill and a real one? They painstakingly study the real bill—every single detail. They can spot a fake bill because they know what the real one looks like. The same is true for words of blessing. Our kids need to be able to recognize the truth spoken in a blessing, versus the lies the world speaks over them. When our kids know deep down inside who they are and where they are headed, anything that contradicts this jumps out at them as untrue. Words of blessing remind our kids about the truth of their identity and destiny.

Whether we want to admit it or not, the enemy does have a plan for our kids' lives. It is very simple and quite effective. His goal is to distort their image of God and their understanding of how God sees them—to isolate them and pull them out of community. Craig Hill in his book *The Ancient Paths*, says that we in North America are the only culture in the world that doesn't have blessing ceremonies naturally built into our cultural system. Look at the Aboriginal people or the Jewish community—each one has natural cultural celebrations and rites of passage that celebrate the worth and value of children and their transitions. Hill likens our North American plight to raising kids in an unwalled city, wide open to the elements and the assaults of a hostile enemy. As parents, when we bless our kids we begin to rebuild the walls that honour and protect them. We take up our role as the spiritual gatekeepers that stand between them and the kingdom of darkness.

We must be intentional about blessing our kids. It needs to be done on purpose, often and consistently. This was part of the Priest's responsibility for the nation of Israel and now our responsibility as priests for our family. We bless our kids so that they will know who they are, Whose they are and where they are headed... their purpose and destiny. We bless them so they will know the truth of how God sees them and the plans He has for their lives. We bless them so that lies won't take root. "When we are subject to spiritual attack through temptation or personal rejection by people who ought to treat us better, it is essential that we know deep down inside who we are in God and where we are going, in order to maintain our perspective. When that truth is embedded in our hearts we are much more successful at keeping lies out."[14]

HOW DO WE BLESS OUR KIDS?

Most of us probably haven't experienced a blessing ourselves and so it is foreign to us. It is also why we miss the significance of it—we don't really know what we are missing. How do you describe a delicious warm cup of coffee to someone who has never tasted or smelled it? How do you explain the value a savoury cup of java brings to your world to someone who doesn't even know it exists? This is kind of how blessing feels to most of us. We are intrigued, and beginning to comprehend the significance of it, but most of us haven't received it or seen it modelled—so how do we learn it?

Practical Tips

How blessing plays out in your family has a lot to do with the personality of your family. It will look similar, but different, based on the temperaments and personalities of your home. Be authentic to who you are. It is often marked by laying on of hands. Studies have been telling us for years about the emotional, healing power of human touch. As believers we have the added element of the Spirit of God that lives within us. When we lay hands on others through prayer, while speaking truth, we become a group conduit of the power of the Holy Spirit. A blessing needs to be spoken out loud, as it breathes life through the vehicle of words. When you bless someone you can have your eyes open and make eye contact or it can be done with eyes closed. You can speak a blessing out over your kids when they are awake or asleep. You are verbally agreeing with Heaven about the truth over your child's identity and purpose.

When James and I first started doing this with our kids it was awkward and uncomfortable and we fumbled our way through it. We chose to persevere because we knew it was important and worthwhile. We were okay with it being awkward for us. Our goal was to make it normal for our kids so that they would be able to pass it on to their children with ease.

In trying to understand blessing, I found that it seemed to be easily divided into three categories: General, Personalized and Significant Occasions.

General Blessings

General blessings are characterized by Scripture verses—truth based on the Bible and God's promises. You may have chosen a special verse for your child when they were born. Speak that out over them. If you haven't done that, ask the Lord to direct you to Scripture specifically for your child. Here are four verses that Mark Holmen recommends in his book, *Take it Home.*[15] They are a great place to start.

Galatians 2:20

"I have been crucified with Christ and I no longer live, but Christ lives in me. The life I now live in the body, I live by faith in the Son of God, who loved me and gave himself for me."[16]

Matthew 5:14, 16

"You are the light of the world. A town built on a hill cannot be hidden. In the same way, let your light shine before others, that they may see your good deeds and glorify your Father in heaven."[17]

Numbers 6:24-26

"The Lord bless you and keep you;
the Lord make his face shine on you and be gracious to you;
the Lord turn his face towards you and give you peace."[18]

Ephesians 3:17-19

"So that Christ may dwell in your hearts through faith. And I pray that you, being rooted and established in love, may have power, together with all the Lord's holy people, to grasp how wide and long and high and deep is the love of Christ, and to know this love that surpasses knowledge—that you may be filled to the measure of all the fullness of God."[19]

The Lord was faithful in placing people and resources across my path as I needed them and researching this topic was no different. I stumbled upon a fantastic book written by a Grandmother for her grandchildren, in the clearance section of our local faith bookstore. *Prayers that avail much, Blessings for Little Ones*, by Germaine Copeland is a book of daily Scripture, promises and truth to speak out over our kids. James used to read an entry to our kids every night before he went to bed. The kids may have been sound asleep, but poignant truth was given life as they rested, through the power of words.

Personalized Blessings

What I am sharing with you in this book initially began as a series of talks and workshops. The first time I taught on this topic, I was challenged to practise what I preached. I knew that I was speaking on blessing and that we had started to do a few things loosely in our family. I knew creating a custom-made blessing for each of my kids was essential, and I wanted to teach others how to do this, but I had no idea how. I knew that it would include some words about their strengths—both natural and learned, as well as their personality and character traits. As I began to pray about it, three simple thoughts came to mind: look at the meaning of their name, ask the Lord for a piece of Scripture for them, and ask Him for a symbol in nature. (See Chapter 7 for more about the symbol in nature.)

Nothing is spoken out over you more than your name and I have a theory about this. My name is Leanne. Leanne means "beautiful one." Every time someone calls me or uses my name—"beautiful one" is spoken over me. Do you know what I have wrestled with most in my life? Feeling beautiful—crazy right? So I shared my theory with a friend of mine and her face got very serious. She went on to tell me that her name means "pure" but the name she heard in her head most of her life was "whore." I wonder if this might give us insight as parents as to what the enemy hurls at our kids. Hannah's name means "God's grace." I wonder if she might struggle with embracing God's grace when she messes up. I wonder if she might wrestle with extending grace to others.

Caleb means "the ability to see the good in others and in difficult situations despite overwhelming odds." I can see the scrimmage in his life over his perspective—seeing the cup as half full or half empty. This gives me such insight in how to intercede for my kids and the truth that needs to be spoken over them.

You might not have chosen your kids' names based on the meaning of the name, or the meaning may not be so affirming. My husband's name, James, means "to take what doesn't belong to you" or "to follow." When I was researching names, the meaning of his deeply bothered me. I was reminded of how the Lord changed Abram's name to Abraham, or how Jacob's name was changed to Israel. I asked the Lord, "What does the name James mean redeemed?" Instantaneously I heard, "to follow faithfully." Anyone who knows my husband would agree that that definition very accurately describes him. Around that same time I was researching my nephew's name for name cards that I was creating for a special occasion and "crooked nose" is what consistently came up. I knew this bothered him as he had told me that before. As I looked a little deeper into the name Cameron, I found that it meant crooked nose because he was a warrior and had fought in so many battles that his nose was permanently crooked. When I gave Cameron his name card, He opened it up and saw "warrior of God" and his face lit up. I could physically see the joy and pride on his face as he embraced and found identity in that meaning. There is power in a name!

What are your hopes and dreams for your child? Ask the Lord how He sees them. Perhaps you might want to include that in their blessing too. Though in our home we speak general blessings out over our kids daily, we speak the personalized blessings out over them once a week.

On Sunday nights our family gathers on the staircase in the centre of our home. James speaks out a blessing over each one of the kids as we all lay hands on each other in agreement. I know this sounds rather "Norman Rockwell" but don't jump to that conclusion. Remember I said that James and I persevered because we knew it was significant? Most Sunday nights, especially when they were little, were brutal. Between accusations of "You're sitting in my spot!" and "You're touching me too hard!" we had to choose not to get distracted by poor behaviour and press on. Today our kids love hearing their blessings (once we are doing it), but getting there can still be a battle. Blessings are rarely convenient and they certainly struggle to compete with all the other options the kids have available to them. So let me encourage you, press on! You are the parents and you get to decide what is best—don't let them wear you down! The opposition is real.

Significant Occasion Blessings
Life transitions and milestones are natural times in a child's life that we have the opportunity to speak words of blessing over them. Baby dedications, baptisms, and choosing to follow Jesus are all such occasions. We have calendar occasions too, like birthdays, Valentine's Day, Family Day, Christmas and Easter. Common life transitions are graduation, weddings and other rites of passage.

After reading a fantastic book by Craig Hill called *The Bar Barakah Blessing*, we decided that we wanted to honour and bless our kids as they transitioned from childhood into adulthood. There are specific things our kids need to hear from us as they enter into adulthood. Each time one of our kids transitions into high school we have a blessing celebration. Friends, family and other adults who have a significant spiritual influence in our kids' lives gather with us over a meal as we all speak words of truth, life, purpose and identity over them. We end the night with a huge party tailored to their personality. For Hannah's we played group Wii Dance, while Caleb chose to have several different gaming stations set up along with a RockBand competition. I can't express to you specifically what happened during each one of those blessings, but what I do know is that the kid who started Grade 9 that year was drastically different from the kid who graduated from Grade 8. Something shifted spiritually as my kids began to embrace the truth spoken over them and as they walked in that. I was ministered to as well, as others pointed out where they saw God at work in my kids' lives.

One of the few times we hear about a person's value, significance and impact is at their funeral. Why do we wait until someone is dead before we affirm God's work in their life? Take advantage of these organic yearly rhythms to speak words of life, identity and destiny over your kids.

Give blessings generously… do not be stingy with your words of life. Words of blessing are like love. Love is not dependent on behaviour or used as a reward… it just *is*. So it is with blessing. Though you may feel tempted to withhold words of blessing when kids are being difficult—this is actually an indication of how desperately they need to hear Godly words of truth, hope, destiny and identity. They need to be reminded of who they are and the incredible future designed for them.

I could wrap this chapter up by summarizing all that we have explored in the last few pages, but I have chosen to leave you with a letter, written by 17-year-old Colten Wilson, about the impact of blessing in his life…

> *"My father's blessing is the single most significant tool that is shaping my young life, keeping me focused on my course in what's ahead. How can a young teen grow into a righteous child of God when he is constantly being bombarded by the world about how to look, what to say, how to fit in and be cool? We have got to know our place, who we are, what we are to be. This is the power of blessing. It is my dad telling me how much he loves me, telling me that I am a man of God—that I am strong, that I am victorious. It is my father speaking over me with his divine authority given to him by God. When I am kneeling in front of my dad, his hands on my head, his eyes looking deep into mine, I can feel his love for me. It is a love that I can never destroy, a love the world can never deprive me of.*
>
> *This love that I get from my father comes from God the Father's love for my dad, which then spills over into my life. Nothing is more life impacting and empowering than that. Bring on the world. I am under the blessing, protection and love of my father.*
>
> *As for me, I'll be passing down the blessing to my children and them to their children, and them to their children. By that time we will have a strong and righteous people under the protection, love and blessing of their parents—a people that God can use to shake nations for His glory. That is the power of the blessing."[20]*

EMBRACING THE GIFT

A Moment to Reflect

- How have I knowingly or unknowingly blessed my children?
- What do we celebrate as a family?
- How can I add words of blessing in our celebrations?
- Who have I hurt with my words?
- Who has hurt me with their words?
- What are two things I can start doing to make blessing a way of life in our family?

Free Gift:
Adding Blessing Elements to Calendar Celebration
Go to: leannecabral.com/book-resources

Chapter 9

Hearing God

Resting on my freshly made bed in the warmth of the early morning sun, I lay with my journal, pen and Bible. What I was reading or studying that morning escapes me but I do recall two littles giggling their way up the stairs and bursting into my room. They climbed their way onto my bed and began jumping. Squealing and chuckling their play quickly turned into a game of chase. I looked at Ella and kindly asked her to take her brother downstairs. "I am almost done," I said, smiling at her. "I can't hear Jesus with you two jumping around up here." I winked. Taking her little brother by the hand she paused and looked up at me a little cock-eyed and then continued out the door.

As I tucked Ella into bed later that evening, she looked up at me and said, "Does God really talk to you mom?" "Yes," I replied, "He does, but not like you hear my voice... When I pray and listen, thoughts come into my head that aren't mine." "Do you think God would talk to me?" she asked. "Why don't you ask Him?" I replied with a grin. With eyes closed tight and in her most sincere three-year-old voice she began to pray, "Dear Jesus, I really want to hear the sound of your voice, can you please talk to me?" We both went quiet for a bit and I began to frantically intercede, "Oh, God she is expecting an audible voice, you have to show up." We waited a little bit longer and I opened my eyes to see if she still had hers closed. She peeked up at me and smiled. "Did you hear anything?" I asked. "Yes," she giggled. "He said I am His princess," she announced with deep conviction.

Kids hear God's voice so easily... so unhindered. We should assume that our kids already hear Him. In his children's book, *Children Can You Hear Me?*, Brad Jersak states that "Children hear the Lord easier than anyone else. Virtually the only block that I encounter in them is their parents' own unbelief."[1] Jersak continues, "The earlier you expect your child to sense God's presence and voice, the less likely you are to shut down their spiritual eyes and ears. Remember that they will be using their imaginations (which can be pretty wild to adult ears), but that is the venue they are providing for Jesus to come. And He will."[2] He tells how his niece meets Jesus on a giant imaginary lollipop and that his son meets Him in a mental petting zoo. "Your initial skepticism will begin to melt as you hear the profound and intimate conversations that ensue."[3]

Some hear Him audibly as Ella did, others hear through their imagination and some hear Him with their hearts—a "knowing." The Bible teaches us that as parents we are to faithfully point our kids to Jesus and help them cultivate an intimate relationship with Him. Part of our assignment is the privilege of helping them to recognize His voice, creating opportunities for them to listen and practise hearing it.

We find ourselves again in this position of "we can't teach what we don't know." So much of this chapter will be about equipping you, so that you can in turn nurture this in your children. My hope for you, dear reader, is this: that you would walk with a greater sense of freedom and understanding in how God has uniquely wired you to commune with Him, and that you would begin to recognize God's voice for yourself if you haven't already, so that you can teach it to your children.

I don't think most of us doubt that God speaks, but I think we sometimes wonder if He would actually speak to us. So let me start with dispelling the myth that God only speaks to a select group of very holy, super-spiritual people. Acts 10: 34 says, "I now realize how true it is that God does not show favouritism."[4] Nothing could be plainer or more clear—God plays no favourites! He is ridiculously partial to each one of us!

Not everyone within the sound of Jesus' voice actually heard Him when He walked the Earth. The ones who heard Him were curious people who sought Him out; those who set aside time to look for Him. Jeremiah 29:13 says that if we seek Him with all our heart, we will be found by Him.[5] When it comes to hearing God I think many already hear Him, but maybe we just haven't recognized His voice or distinguished it from all the other voices and noise that compete for our time and attention. Learning to discern God's voice takes practice.

SACRED PATHWAYS

Gary Thomas, a well known U.S. pastor and author, wrote a fantastic book called *Sacred Pathways*. Thomas was frustrated in his own quiet times with the Lord. He longed for more as he felt his devotional life was getting a little stale. Out of that place of longing, a book emerged as he decided to lean in. "All too often Christians who desire to be fed spiritually are given the same generic hopefully all-inclusive methods—usually some variation on a standardized quiet time. Why, because it is simple, it's generic and it is easy to hold people accountable to—but for many Christians it is just not enough."[6] God has created us with a certain personality and a certain spiritual temperament. God wants us to worship and commune with Him according to the way He has made us. So Thomas began to study how people in Scripture and church history connected with God. He began to see nine different, but equally valued temperaments emerge.

Naturalist: Loving God through nature – King David

Sensates: Loving God with the senses – King Solomon

Traditionalists: Loving God through ritual and symbol – Abraham

Ascetics: Loving God through silence and solitude and simplicity – John the Baptist

Activists: Loving God through confrontation – Moses and James

Caregivers: Loving God by loving others – Mordecai and Luke

Enthusiasts: Loving God with mystery and celebration – Miriam

Contemplatives: Loving God through adoration – Mary, at the feet of Jesus

Intellectuals: Loving God with the mind – Solomon and John

Jesus welcomed the worship of Peter's mother-in-law as she served Him, but didn't force Mary the sister of Martha to worship Him in that same way. Mary was allowed to sit at His feet and worship Him in the silence of adoration. Understanding our own personal temperaments tells us how we relate to others, but knowing our spiritual temperaments helps us understand how we relate to God so we can develop new ways of drawing near to Him.[7]

 Free Gift: Discover your Own Spiritual Pathway
Go to: leannecabral.com/book-resources

CREATING AN ATMOSPHERE TO HEAR GOD

Knowing your sacred pathway will play a key role in determining the most favourable environment for you to hear God. Think about what inspires you, what naturally draws you close to Him. For those who love nature, outdoors may be a first choice. For those who are contemplative, a quiet spot with little distraction may be ideal.

When we are first learning to discern God's voice it is important that we quiet the noise around us and silence the other voices that compete against God's still small voice. Environmental noises like phones, TV and music may be a distraction. According to Scripture there are three voices that compete against the voice of God. In Ephesians 2, Paul refers to them as the flesh, the world and the devil. All three were present in the Garden of Eden at the time of Adam and Eve's temptation, and we still deal with these same voices today. Our own voice—our own internal thinking and rationalization. The voice of others—words spoken by family, friends, coworkers and the media. The voice of the enemy—satan and his demons.

How do we quiet these voices? We pray and ask for Jesus' help. When I am trying to listen to the voice of God I pray something like this…

> "Lord Jesus Christ,
>
> In this moment, I surrender myself to you the best way
> that I know how—especially my own thoughts and voice.
> I ask you Lord Jesus to deal with the voices of other people
> and the enemy on my behalf. Please bind up, silence and
> remove all that is not of you, Lord Jesus, from me and
> this place now. I ask for your complete protection Lord,
> especially for the full armour of God to be placed upon
> me now… the helmet of salvation, the breastplate of
> righteousness, the belt of truth, the gospel of peace upon
> my feet, the shield of faith and the sword of the Spirit. Please
> cleanse me of all sin and align me to you now Holy Spirit. In
> the name of Jesus Christ of Nazareth—Amen"

After these voices are quieted, it is much easier to discern God's voice.

Techniques to Quiet Your Mind

If you are having trouble quieting your mind, try some of these ideas:

1. Get a pad of paper and as your mind wanders to things that need to get done, write them down as a way of quieting your mind, until things settle.
2. Close your eyes and take deep breaths. Inhale for four counts and exhale for four counts—this actually slows down the internal workings of your body.
3. Sometimes bringing your internal talk down to one word or phrase by focusing on God and saying "You are Holy"

or "Redeemer" is helpful. It is like the decrescendo bringing it right down to silence.

Once you feel quiet inside, ask the Lord one question like: "Is there anything you want to say to me Lord Jesus?" Pause and listen for a response. If nothing comes, wait and persist. Thoughts will often surface to the forefront of your mind. Don't censor them, instead write them down and test them later.

CHALLENGES TO HEARING GOD'S VOICE

Sometimes there are things in our life that can make hearing God's voice difficult. **Unconfessed sin** can be a barrier to hearing Him. Keep short accounts with God; when we mess up, be quick to make it right. Sometimes our **attitude, preconceived ideas or false beliefs** can stand in the way. Submit them to Christ and allow Him to work them out with you. I think one of the largest obstacles to recognizing His voice is **busyness**. We live such fast-paced, full lives, we often don't have room to "be still and know." It is essential that we learn to slow life down, to live life with enough margin for us to wait for Him and listen for His still small voice. **Un-forgiveness** could stand in our way too. Forgiveness is a process and sometimes it is about being willing to begin that process with a God who desperately loves us and wants His best for us. **Warped views** can also impede our ability to hear His voice. A warped view of self and a warped view of God marked my life and I wrote about it in the beginning of the book. Let me encourage you, Jeremiah 29:12 so clearly tells us that when we seek Him with all our heart, we will be found by Him.[8] That is exactly what happened to me. It was as I sought Him that He began to unravel my warped views, and if you struggle with this,

He will do it for you too. **Past hurt or disappointment** can also make it difficult to hear Him. Our woundedness can distort our filter, yet choosing to walk through pain is often the first step to unleashing our own potential. It is in our area of pain that we often stumble into our greatest area of influence. Ask the Lord to reveal anything to you that might prevent you from hearing Him. Don't go searching for it, let the Holy Spirit bring it to mind. If He does, give it to Jesus and have a chat about it.

HOW DO I KNOW IT IS GOD SPEAKING?

This really is *the* question, right? It requires us to know the truth about God. What we believe about God and ourselves will greatly impact our ability to hear God clearly.

A friend tells a story about how she was praying with a woman. The woman was having a hard time speaking out the truth she heard from the Lord. My friend encouraged her to write down whatever she was hearing—without editing it. You see God was bringing this phrase to the woman's mind, "You are delightful." Do you know why she was struggling with this truth? Because she had grown up with a verbally abusive father who regularly criticized her and put her down. Her earthly father never delighted in her and because of her past she could not believe that her Heavenly Father could possibly delight in her either.

Do you see how God may be speaking to us but our own filters or beliefs may distort and even block us from clearly understanding God's thoughts towards us? Now there was a breakthrough for this woman and she was able to stop being the judge of herself and allow God to be the judge of her. So often God speaks tender, positive, affirming words to us and we can't believe He would ever think that way about us because we don't think that way about ourselves. We must stop being the judge of ourselves and let Him be the one who defines us. Not others, not ourselves—allow Him to redefine you.

Have you ever heard a series of jokes that start with "you know you're a Canadian when…"? Well my dear friend Beth Graf came up with a similar routine about hearing God's voice.

You Know it's God Speaking When…
- **What you sense aligns with Scripture.** God will never say anything that contradicts His Holy Word.
- **What He says aligns with His character.** If you ever wonder about God's character, check out the famous love passage in 1 Corinthians 13. If God is love then all of these attributes of love are also attributes of God's character. If you are trying to hear God's voice and words come to you that sound like nagging, scolding or words of accusation that make you feel guilt-ridden—it's not God. God's Spirit challenges us. He convicts us, but in the distinct absence of guilt and shame. There will be genuine remorse, but He is always kind and courteous. Scripture says that it is *His kindness that leads us to repentance*. If you are feeling accused or condemned, that is what the Bible calls satan, the accuser.
- **What you sense is accompanied by peace and rest**—a settledness in your spirit. God is not the author of confusion or agitation. He is called the Prince of Peace.
- **What you sense might be a new truth or revelation or**

epiphany (always aligning with Scripture). It may be a deeper insight to a truth you already know. I live by the lake and I was out walking one stormy Saturday morning. After strolling in the wind and rain for half an hour I decided to turn around and head back. As I turned around it became apparently obvious that I had been walking with the wind the entire time. Now I was being assaulted by horizontal rain and I really couldn't see. I was dodging snails as the rain seemed to bring them out onto the path in multitudes. It was exhausting. I was tired so I decided to just close my eyes and trust the Lord to lead me on this path… and kindly asked him not to let me step on any more snails. This became such a tangible lesson that in the midst of the storm, when you cannot see a way out, close your eyes and trust the One who sees the path in perfect clarity.

- **What you sense might cause you to wrestle internally**. Moses is such a great example of this in Exodus 3 and 4. When God spoke to Moses in the burning bush and called him to lead His people out of Egypt, Moses gave God every excuse why he couldn't. He wrestled with God and questioned Him—"Are you sure you have the right person for this job? What if I go and the people don't believe that you sent me? I stutter and I don't speak eloquently." Like Moses, when the right thing to do comes to mind and yet I find myself arguing it in my head—this is a big clue to me that the Holy Spirit is prompting me.
- **What you think God is saying to you is confirmed externally by others or situations**. Always make sure you test what others say or what you experience. Make sure it aligns with Scripture and God's character.

Sometimes we think God will give us some grandiose word when in reality it may be a very simple instruction or insight. He may only give you a word like *rest* or a simple instruction like *pick up that cup and throw it out*. God's voice and His words to us are often not what we expect. In 1 Kings 19 the Lord passes by Elijah who is standing on a mountain. Elijah was expecting God to be in the whirlwind, the earthquake, and then the fire, but instead God was in a gentle whisper.

LISTENING OPPORTUNITIES WITH OUR KIDS

Omnipresent

Because God is always with us, here are some great questions you can ask your child. Where do you see God in this room? What is He doing? What does He look like? Is He saying anything to you? Are there any angels with Him?

Because God loves to talk to us, ask your children—What is God telling you? What is He showing you? How is He feeling?

Bedtime

Bedtime is a great time to practise listening. After your child finishes their prayer, have them ask the Lord if there is anything else He wants to say to them. Go quiet and wait a few minutes. As they begin to share what they heard or saw, record it in their Bible. A friend of mine put poster board above her kids' beds and each time they heard a word from the Lord, she wrote it down on the poster board for them.

Bad Dreams

Bad dreams or nightmares are also an opportunity to hear God. Invite Him in to defuse the situation. Ask the Lord to come into the bad dream or into the room and deal with whatever is there. Another friend tells a story about her son who had a bad dream. "I went into Nate's room as he was calling me. He said that he had a bad dream and that he was afraid. So I said to him, 'Let's ask Jesus to come into your dream.'" Her son prayed and invited Jesus to do just that. She proceeded to ask him, "Is Jesus in your dream?" "Yes," he answered. "Where is He in your dream?" she asked. He told her where he saw Jesus. She encouraged him to ask Jesus to deal with his bad dream or to take it away. He began to laugh as he told his mom that Jesus was kicking the monster in the bum and that it was yelping and running away. They laughed and thanked Jesus together and went back to sleep.

Quarrels

Taking disputes at home or at school to Jesus is also a great opportunity to listen to Him. Ask your child questions like: What happened? How did that make you feel? Where was Jesus when this happened? Is He saying anything to you? Do you need His help to stop feeling sad or angry about what happened? Is there anything you need to ask forgiveness for? Does Jesus have anything else to say to you about this situation?

Emotions

When our kids feel sad or afraid we have an opportunity to listen. Have them picture a great big blanket in their mind. Ask them to share with you what they are afraid of or what is causing them to feel sad. Ask them to place each fear or thing that makes them sad on the blanket. Invite them to ask Jesus to come and get the blanket and to take it away. Have them ask Jesus if there is anything He wants to say to them about their fears or sadness. Ask Him if He wants to give them anything to replace the fear or sadness.

LISTENING ACTIVITIES FOR OUR KIDS

Art

Set out canvases or paper and paints for your family. Before you begin, pray something like this: "Lord Jesus, you are Creator and because we are created in your image we also have the privilege of creating. If creation itself calls out to you, would you speak to us today as we explore our own creativity." Once the family has finished and the painting has dried, invite Jesus to speak to each of you through your art. Ask four questions:

1. What catches your eye in this piece of art work?
2. Ask Jesus why He is showing it to you.
3. Ask Jesus if there is anything He wants to say to you about you or about Himself through this piece of art.
4. Ask Him if there is anything else He wants to say.

Images or Sketches

I googled "pencil sketches of Jesus with children" and printed several of them out. I asked each person to choose their favourite image. We prayed and invited Jesus to join us and speak to us through the art in front of us. We asked four questions:

1. What do I love about this image or why did I choose it?
2. What do You want to say to me about me through this picture?
3. What do You want to say to me about You through this picture?
4. Is there anything else You would like to say to me about this?

Soaking

Allow your family to get settled in a position that is physically comfortable for them. Pass out some paper and pencil crayons. Play some worship music and as the music washes over, have each person draw or write down words, thoughts or images that come to their mind. Once the music is finished, ask the Lord if there is anything else He has to say.

Chocolate

Give each person a piece of chocolate. Tell them they cannot chew it, but to let it melt in their mouth until it disappears. Once the chocolate has melted away ask these questions:

1. Describe the experience of letting chocolate dissolve in your mouth
2. How is God's love like a piece of chocolate?
3. What does God want to tell you about His love through a piece of chocolate?
4. How does God want you to show the sweetness of His love to others?
5. How does God want you to show the sweetness of love to yourself?

Nature

Place a vase of flowers in the centre of your table. Give each person a piece of paper and a pen. Ask the following questions:

1. Describe what you see.
2. What is the purpose of a flower?
3. After reviewing your first two answers, What does God have to say to you, about you, through a little flower?

Lectio Divina

Read a Bible story to your kids. After reading it the first time invite them to ask Jesus to give them a word, thought or image as you read it again. Next have them ask the Lord, "Why are You showing me this?" as you read it a third time. Have them ask the Lord, "Is there anything You are asking me to do?" as you read it a final time.

Contemplative

Read a Bible story to your kids. After reading it, have them ask Jesus who they are in the story. Read it again. Now ask Jesus, "What do You want to say about me through this character?" Read it a third time and then ask Jesus, "What do You want to say to me about You through this story or this character?" Read the story a final time and ask the Lord if there is anything else He would like to say.

Friends, you are wired for this! He has created you uniquely, and designed you to commune with Him. Recognizing God's voice in my own life was instrumental in cultivating an intimate relationship with Him. As we intentionally create space for God in our lives and our kids, we will learn to not only see, but experience the Lord in the everyday circumstances of life. He is speaking—will you make room to listen? I can think of no greater gift to give our kids!

EMBRACING THE GIFT

A Moment to Reflect

- What is stirring within you after reading this chapter?
- Explore and discover how God has uniquely designed you to hear His voice.
- What can you do to feed your spiritual pathway?
- What is one thing you would like to do in your family, to help your kids recognize His voice?

Chapter 10

Spiritual Protection

"**M**om...mom...mom," a wee voice whispered in the early hours of the morning. I struggled to open my eyes and focus on the face two inches from mine. "Yes buddy, what's the matter?" I asked. "I had a bad dream... can you pray for me?" "Sure," I replied to the frightened four-year-old standing in footed flannels. I asked the true Lord Jesus Christ of Nazareth to wash over him and remove all that was not of Him from our home now. I asked the Lord to meet Caleb in his thoughts and dreams and for His peace to fall upon him and to give him sweet rest. Caleb went back to his room. I flipped my pillow over, pulled up the duvet and began to nod off as I heard his little feet coming back to my side of the bed again. "Yes sweetheart," I said. "It's still there mom... can you pray in my room?" I got out of bed, scooped him up and brought him back to his bedroom. I prayed again... this time I added, "If there is anything here from the kingdom of darkness, you need to leave now in Jesus' name." Kissing his cheek, I tucked him back into bed. I had barely gotten back into my bed when he walked back in and announced, "It's still there, mom." I told him to crawl into bed with us. I turned over as he wiggled himself between James and me. Drifting off to sleep I felt a little finger tapping me on the shoulder. "Mom, it's here," he said. Turning towards him, I replied, "Buddy, wake up your dad and ask him to pray." He woke up his dad and James prayed a half-asleep kind of prayer commanding anything unholy to leave this space now in Jesus' name. No sooner had the words left his mouth, the three of us fell into a deep, restful sleep.

Caleb often struggled with bad dreams. As a toddler, he could very accurately describe the terror that woke him up. With eyes wide open, he would point to things visible to him… things we couldn't see, but he could describe in detail. We weren't really sure what to do about it and initially wrote it off as a vivid imagination. Though imagination may have been a part of it, there seemed to be more. We weren't equipped to deal with his night terrors, nor did we fully understand the source from which they came.

Part of passing faith on to our kids is talking to them about the battle between the Kingdom of God and the kingdom of darkness, teaching our kids how to guard themselves and stand their ground against an enemy they cannot see. However, we can't teach our kids what we don't know ourselves. We can't pass tools on to them we haven't yet learned. This is where I found myself, in this odd space of "I don't know." I needed to figure some of this out so that I could more effectively pass it on to my kids.

I grew up in a home that acknowledged the kingdom of darkness, but rarely spoke of it. I felt that I lacked experience, ability and understanding when it pertained to these kinds of things. During this season the Lord placed us in a church, a conservative church, that was willing to have these kinds of conversations and unpack this loaded subject in a healthy, balanced and Biblically rooted way. My desire was to better understand the spiritual realm and to figure out the tools and authority God had given us as believers as we guarded ourselves, our home and our family.

During this time, the Lord kept bringing a verse to mind: "For God has not given you a spirit of fear and timidity, but of power, love and self-discipline" (2 Timothy 1:7).[1] Exploring this subject was not about being afraid of all that I did not see or understand, but about embracing the authority, identity and position that I, have as a child of the Most High God. It is an authority that all of us possess when we claim Jesus as Lord.

THEORY

I have noticed that many shy away from this conversation or feel unsettled with this topic. I think we sometimes feel fearful of what we do not know or understand. Perhaps we are afraid of swinging so far to the other side of this conversation that we may begin to sound paranoid or a little crazy. But I want to have a balanced, honest conversation about this while looking at Scripture and our faith history. One that is authentic and maybe a little messy. One from a position of assurance, not fear. As it has been said before, we can't change what we don't acknowledge or understand, so let's lean into this a bit. My pastor, Dr. Jon Thompson, wrote his dissertation on this topic and much of what I share with you comes from his research, insight and teachings, as I have sat under his instruction and served with him.[2]

Old Testament

Throughout Scripture there is a gradual unveiling of a cosmic battle between a Holy God and evil. We see it in the Garden of Eden and in the Fall as satan tempts Eve. In the story of Job, satan walks into God's presence challenging Him about His servant Job. The Old

Testament is saturated with stories about the gods of the nations and Yahweh, God of the Israelites. Through the Old Testament we begin to understand that the universe is not just God, the animal kingdom and those made in the image of the Creator—there is another part that is invisible to most. Daniel 10:4-21 reveals that an Angel sent to answer Daniel's prayer was held up in battle against the prince of Persia for 21 days until the Angel Michael came to relieve him. 2 Kings 6:15-17 tells the story of Elisha's servant who was terrified when he saw an army with horses and chariots surrounding the city. Elisha prayed for the Lord to open his servant's eyes and when he opened his eyes he saw the invisible part of the world where the hills were full of horses and chariots of fire.

New Testament

The New Testament continues to reveal this cosmic battle. The Gospel of John theologically outlines the world possessed by the kingdom of darkness. Satan is called the "prince of this world" in John three times, making the birth of a Saviour an act of invasion. These kingdom clashes continue through the New Testament, as satan tempts Jesus in the wilderness. Dr. Thompson states, "There is a pattern found in the gospels—Jesus would preach, evil would manifest in people, Jesus would rebuke the evil spirits and the tormented men, women and children would be set free."[3] At the resurrection, Jesus overcomes the kingdom of darkness and the book of Acts begins. The ministry of Jesus and His acts continue through His Holy Spirit. The apostles continue to build the church and there is a sub-theme of conflict or "turf wars."[4] Every time there is an advancement of the gospel in a new area, there is always a confrontation with the demonic. As you delve into Revelation it is clear that there is a cosmic battle that has happened, is happening and will happen.

Revelation 17:13-14

> *"They have one purpose and will give their power and authority to the beast. They will wage war against the Lamb, but the Lamb will triumph over them because he is Lord of lords and King of kings—and with him will be his called, chosen and faithful followers."[5]*

Church History

Our faith history has also documented these spiritual battles. In his dissertation Dr. Thompson says, "There is a living history of a variety of church leaders dealing with the demonic not only in the areas of theology but also pastorally as people came needing freedom."[6] By the second century the act of baptism and exorcism would join together because most of those becoming christians were converting from pagan religions and needed an act of deliverance to deal with other spiritual influences. Right through the Great Schism, when the Christian Church divided into the Greek Orthodox and Roman Catholic branches, it is fascinating to note that both continued the practice of exorcism instituted by the first, second and third century church leaders. For those of us who are Protestant, it is interesting to see that great leaders like Martin Luther and John Wesley record encounters with the demonic. Even Charles Swindoll wrote a book on this subject called *Freedom from Spiritual Bondage*.

As Western Christians many of us struggle with the reality of the spirit realm. Most North American Christians would agree they believe that what the Bible says is true about satan and his demons. I think the challenge for most of us is that while we would agree with the Biblical reality of the kingdom of darkness, we struggle with how to address it in our everyday lives.

PRACTICAL

As I began to understand a bit more about the active involvement of the demonic realm through Scripture and church history, I began to see how it played out in my life and in my family too. I believe in a balanced holistic approach to this subject. There are many parts that make us up. We are physical, emotional, mental, social and spiritual and we need to look at all of these elements as we explore this. Is it possible that Caleb had an overactive imagination? Yes. Is it plausible that he was overtired and experienced an element of sensory deprivation where in the dark, your mind creates images? Maybe. Could he be lucid dreaming? Possibly. But when he is fully awake and still seeing or feeling a presence that a typical four-year-old can't explain, could it be something more? Again, maybe. I wanted to understand this spiritual piece on a practical level. I wanted to know about the tools and authority we've been given as children of God to guard ourselves, our homes and our family.

It was a normal midweek afternoon. The kids came home from school, ate their snack and were off doing their own thing. Caleb was pretty quiet that afternoon. He wasn't a big talker and I had gotten used to asking him a lot of questions to draw him out. That afternoon though he was especially mellow. After several questions it became clear that a kid at school was giving him a hard time and pushing him down each time he went out for recess and came back in.

I asked him who it was and he shrugged his shoulders. So I

continued, "Do you not recognize him? Is he a kid in another Grade 2 class? Is he an older kid? Have you ever seen him before?" Each question was met with an "I don't know" response. Since the incidents took place at recess I asked him what other classes exit the same door as him. He still shrugged his shoulders. Unsure of where to go from here it dawned on me to ask him, "Where are your eyes looking when you are walking?" "On the floor," he responded. No wonder he didn't know who it was... he truly didn't see him.

I quickly realized that I was going to have to coach him step by step on how to stand up for himself—how to guard himself. Beginning with the first step, I said to him, "Caleb, from now on whenever you walk, I want you to look everyone in the eye so you can see who is around you. Next, when you see someone extend their arm to push you down, I want you to set both feet firmly on the ground, look them straight in the eye, lower the tone of your voice and firmly say: *'Don't push me!'*" We practised this a few times and on the way to school the next day I again reminded him of what to do.

"It works!! It works!!" Caleb exclaimed, bursting through the door that afternoon. "What works?" I asked. "I did what you told me to. I looked everybody in the eye and when I saw the kid start to push me, I put my feet down on the floor, used my deep voice and said: *'Don't push me!'* And the kid walked away," he blurted, exploding with pride and confidence.

Just as Caleb needed to be coached step by step about how to guard himself, so I too, had to be coached on how to guard myself, my home and my family from a very different bully.

Guarding Ourselves

As I wrote earlier, my friend Beth Graf, who is the prayer pastor at our church, was quick to teach me that authority over powers of darkness is entry-level Christianity—as soon as you receive Christ, you've got it. This authority isn't something we earn, it is bestowed to us. However, spiritual gifts, position and divine appointment can play a role in the measure of authority we have.[7] Just like in an army, a general has greater authority by position than a foot soldier. A pastor strictly by position carries a different authority than a lay person. Did you notice in the story about Caleb in the beginning of the chapter that I as his mom prayed three times and nothing seemed to change? Did you see how when James, the spiritual head of our home prayed, it was immediate? We all have authority over the powers of darkness because of the Holy Spirit in us, but our allotment isn't always equal.[8]

Spiritual oppression can take on many different faces. Sometimes it appears as fear or terror, or as a terrible dream. Others feel like they are being watched or followed. For myself it often manifested through condemning third person accusations in my head. Some people have trouble in a worship service or when they are reading Scripture or taking communion. Other times it may appear as persistent negative thoughts or an "off" perspective. Maybe family strife is magnified or weakness heightened. Like Caleb choosing to look up, we have to recognize what oppression looks like in our life so we can stand against it. Once we see or feel it coming we choose our next steps, and the tools we want to use to guard ourselves and stand our ground. Here are a few tools that I found really helpful not only in my own life, but also in teaching and equipping my kids.

Tool #1 – Spiritual Armour
Ephesians 6:11-17

> *"Put on the full armour of God, so that you can take your
> stand against the devil's schemes. For our struggle is not
> against flesh and blood, but against the rulers, against the
> authorities, against the powers of this dark world and against
> the spiritual forces of evil in the heavenly realms. Therefore
> put on the full armour of God, so that when the day of evil
> comes, you may be able to stand your ground, and after you
> have done everything, to stand. Stand firm then, with the
> belt of truth buckled round your waist, with the breastplate
> of righteousness in place, and with your feet fitted with the
> readiness that comes from the gospel of peace. In addition
> to all this, take up the shield of faith, with which you can
> extinguish all the flaming arrows of the evil one. Take the
> helmet of salvation and the sword of the Spirit, which is the
> word of God."*[9]

Notice it says *when* the day of evil comes... not *if*. We should
expect opposition, and we should expect to have to fight. I think
the armour is both figurative and literal. It is a great reminder of
holy living and in our home we actually pray on our armour daily
as a family when I drive the kids to school.

Tool #2 – Keep Short Accounts with God
We are prone to wander. As much as we want to live holy,
righteous lives we find ourselves entangled in sin all the time. This
is part of living in a fallen world and our very real wrestle with sin.
Ephesians 4:26-27 says, "And don't sin by letting anger control
you. Don't let the sun go down while you are still angry, for anger

gives a foothold to the devil."[10] The word *foothold*[11] in this verse actually conveys spatial language in the original Greek, meaning that in our unconfessed sin, we give actual room or space for the enemy to be. When we sin, be quick to make things right again with the Lord. We can't allow room for the enemy to linger.

Tool #3 – Be Quick to Forgive.

Forgiveness is a vast and loaded subject that I can't delve into deeply, but there are a few things I want to highlight. Forgiveness doesn't necessarily mean reconciliation. We can work through forgiveness without having a relationship restored. I am not advocating blanket forgiveness either. I think forgiveness is a process we work through and it is about being willing to begin that process with an ever-loving God. Romans 12:18 says, "As far as it is up to you, live at peace with everyone."[12] We must honour and guard our vertical relationship with God, even if it doesn't always translate to repaired relationships horizontally.

Tool #4 – Spiritual Disciplines

We need to embrace and practise spiritual disciplines. **Prayer**, both listening and speaking, is instrumental in guarding ourselves. "Therefore confess your sins to each other and pray for each other so that you may be healed. The prayer of a righteous person is powerful and effective."[13] (James 5:16)

We need to saturate ourselves in **Scripture**. Joshua 1:8 says, "Keep this Book of the Law always on your lips; meditate on it day and night, so that you may be careful to do everything written in it. Then you will be prosperous and successful."[14] We need to know Him and know His Word. How else will we know truth from lies? Jesus used Scripture each time He was tempted, to combat the enemy. I have often referred to Zechariah 3:2 when I confront the enemy: "The One who has chosen Leanne rebukes you—now be silent."[15]

We must immerse ourselves in **community** with other believers. Being a part of the local church is not only a great idea, it is required of us who follow Jesus.

Acts 2:44-47

"All the believers were together and had everything in common. They sold property and possessions to give to anyone who had need. Every day they continued to meet together in the temple courts. They broke bread in their homes and ate together with glad and sincere hearts, praising God and enjoying the favour of all the people. And the Lord added to their number daily those who were being saved."[16]

Being a part of a community of believers places us under the spiritual protection of the local church too—we fall under the shelter of their umbrella.

Tithing is another way we stand our ground and guard ourselves from the enemy.

Malachi 3:10-12

"Bring the full tithe into the storehouse, that there may be food in my house. And thereby put me to the test, says the Lord of hosts, if I will not open the windows of heaven for you and pour down for you a blessing until there is no more need. I will rebuke the devourer for you, so that it will not

destroy the fruits of your soil, and your vine in the field shall not fail to bear, says the Lord of hosts. Then all nations will call you blessed, for you will be a land of delight, says the Lord of hosts."[17]

Please don't misunderstand me, I am not saying we buy our protection. I am saying that tithing is a physical demonstration of where and to Whom our allegiance lies. We give our first fruits to our God and He says He will rebuke the devourer. It doesn't mean that if we don't tithe the Lord doesn't protect us, rather if the oppression is intense, we do need to take a look at our life and see if any fences are down. Tithing is a fence.

In all of this we must look at personal responsibility, too. We can't blame satan for every calamity in our lives. We can't use him as an excuse for our poor behaviour. We do have personal responsibility for our emotions, and our own mental and physical health. We need to look at the organic struggles in our lives. Am I tired? Am I hungry? Look at this in the balance of all that makes us up—wholeness.

Guarding our Home

Our living space is an extension of ourselves—our home is another battlefield the enemy likes to drop in on. The assault in our homes isn't alway an overt one. I wonder if his plot is more subtle, one where we can almost think it's us. Here are some scenarios my friend Beth describes—see if any of these resonate with you…

You arrive home after a great day out. You are happy and energized—excited to embrace family life. As you exit your car and walk in the front door "all hell breaks loose." You go from excited to exasperated, delighted to defeated—from elated to anger in a matter of seconds...

Or, you are in your home joyfully puttering away feeling content. As you enter the basement strange thoughts enter you mind... depressing, fear-filled ones. You get spooked and head upstairs...

Sometimes strife happens in our homes for no good reason and arguments flare over nothing. You find yourself nit-picking, nagging and criticizing. Joy is robbed and peace turns to chaos...

Perhaps on Sunday mornings as you get your family ready for church you find that friction, quarrels and bickering swell up. Doesn't it make sense that the enemy would try to wreck us just before we go to God's house?

We can save ourselves much unnecessary distress by faithfully guarding our homes. How do we do that? We pray. We pray *initially* and *continuously*. In Chapter 6 we explored *initially*, the importance of praying through our home and dedicating it to Jesus. But how do we *continue* to maintain it? Just like in any war all ground reclaimed from the enemy must be vigilantly protected and guarded from future assaults. So too, our enemy doesn't stop trying to harass and gain entrance. The difference is that now a wall has been established and borders have been defined making it much more difficult for the enemy to enter. Caleb had to *continue* to look up and look people straight in the eye to be aware of his surroundings so that he could guard himself if needed.

We maintain what has been reclaimed by praying, especially when we sense or feel promptings from the Holy Spirit. We get used to the freedom and light and we become more sensitive to the tactics of the kingdom of darkness. When we live in an atmosphere of peace we are more keenly aware when chaos emerges out of nowhere. It becomes a trigger for us to pray. Sometimes we don't know what or how to pray. I would love to give you some prayers that have been really helpful to our family. They are great maintenance prayers and jumping-off points when we don't know what to pray.

 Free Gift: Prayers.
Go to: leannecabral.com/book-resources

Another tool for guarding our home is to pray after guests or family have been over, as they may have come with their own spiritual baggage. After they leave we make a simple declaration that we only accept what is good and Godly from our time together with them and that all else must depart now in Jesus' name and never return.

Maintenance prayers are not difficult and don't need to be long. Like any habit that we begin and practise, it becomes a part of our daily routine and we get used to it.

Guarding our Family
This is a tricky one as it isn't specifically or topically addressed in Scripture. As I was praying about it and the subject was ruminating in my mind, a few thoughts came to me. Thoughts about how as parents we can stand between the kingdom of darkness and our children, and how we can equip our kids to stand for themselves "when the day of evil comes."[18] (Ephesians 6:13)

We guard our family through prayer. As we intercede for them we can stand between them and the enemy through prayer. We can ask the Lord specifically what to pray for our kids. He knit them together, He knows what their struggles are and where the enemy will seek to gain influence in their lives.

We can model to our kids how to pray when we feel oppression. When Ella was little she was afraid to go into the basement. She would take my hand and make me go with her. I did this for a while, and then one day it struck me to pray out loud for her. I simply said, "Jesus is with us, we will not be afraid." After a while she began to say it with me. One day she called me again to go to the basement with her and I encouraged her to try on her own—that Jesus is with her. From the kitchen I could here her little three-year-old voice intently repeating, "Jesus is with me, I will not be afraid," over and over again, as she bravely tackled the basement stairs by herself.

This is also why Caleb knew to get us to pray for him when he had nightmares. When he was little we could comfort him, pray out loud and sing worship music over him until he settled. Praying because of bad dreams became a knee-jerk response for him... an equipping.

Teaching our kids to hear God's voice is another essential tool of equipping for our kids and guarding our family. As I wrote in Chapter 9, learning to hear God's voice for themselves is instrumental. As they begin to recognize His voice and the characteristics of it, they are quick to learn what is not His voice. They learn to hear truth directly from the source, allowing them to distinguish between the voice of the enemy and the voice of

God. They know the difference between the two. Creating space to practise hearing God's voice can shape a lifelong habit of listening. It cultivates a confidence and boldness in their prayers.

After prayer with your children allow time to listen. Have your children ask the Lord if there is anything else He would like to say to them. When I started doing this with my own kids, I began to date and document what they heard in the blank pages of their devotional Bibles.

We have a box of old photo Christmas cards from friends and family. Every so often we pull it out and each of us chooses a picture. Before we pray for the family in front of us, we have a few minutes of silence where we ask the Lord what to pray for each family.

These are small quick exercises that cultivate an atmosphere to hear God's voice. Chapter 9 is a whole chapter dedicated to teaching our kids to hear God's voice and the practical application of it.

Words of blessing is another way that we as parents can guard our Family. As we saw in the previous chapter on blessing, we can use our words to speak life, identity and purpose over our kids. These words of blessing remind our children of who they are and the incredible plans God has for them. Blessing is a profound way to guard our kids against the lies of the enemy and the world. When they know what is true about them, as they have heard it spoken out over them time and time again, they are quick to see something that contradicts. They recognize it for the lie that it is. When they hear a lie and see it for what it is, they can use the words of blessing they have heard spoken out over them along with Scripture to combat the lie. Truth and Scripture are quick weapons to silence the enemy. Our kids become equipped to do exactly what Jesus did in the wilderness when satan tempted him, they stand their ground by speaking truth to the enemy.

I appreciate your willingness to delve into a subject that can make some feel a little vulnerable and uncomfortable. It is a significant conversation about the reality of our faith. A conversation that needs to be had, because as we wrestle our way through it, God begins to teach us and equip us. As we trust His leading and begin to understand more, we stand a little taller and a walk a little bolder. Coming to terms with the reality of this subject and seeing how it plays out in our own lives, we can choose to walk in the authority He has bestowed to us and embrace the tools He has given as we guard ourselves, our homes and our family.

EMBRACING THE GIFT

A Moment to Reflect

- What is stirring within you after reading this?
- Is there anything you need to take to Jesus?
- Ask the Lord to show you where the enemy is seeking to gain ground in your family.
- What is one thing you can start doing to guard your family?

Chapter 11

A Family Who Serves Together...

In an overcrowded coffee shop with a warm cup of deliciousness in my hands, I sat across from a new friend. Her eyes welled up as she began to recount a story of her tenderhearted son, who had a "Jesus-sized" dose of mercy and compassion trapped inside a middle school boy's body. Her son was physically moved by the homeless people he passed when they visited downtown. Full of questions and with deep concern, he asked his mom, where do they live?…Where will they sleep?…How will they eat?…How will they get warmer clothes? With incredible wisdom, my new friend didn't shy away from her son's difficult questions. She recognized a look in his eyes that compelled her to pay attention and lean in.

A few days later she contacted a friend who worked with street youth in the city. Knowing her son wouldn't fit the qualifications to volunteer because of his age, she asked if there was a homeless youth he could pray for. For the next two weeks, her son diligently interceded for a stranger named Frankie. He wrote the boy's name in a prayer journal he made with his mom. Every night at bedtime he would ask God to help Frankie, to save him, and to give him hope. They weren't long prayers, just ones that brought

Frankie before the Lord. Two weeks later, their phone rang saying that Frankie had just committed his life to Jesus. Her son had an opportunity to speak to Frankie that night—he was dumbfounded that an 11-year-old in the suburbs was praying for him.

Aaron, my new friend's son, continued to intercede for kids on the streets by name. One evening he was invited to travel with the team who worked with homeless youth and meet Frankie and other street youth he was praying for so they could put a face to his name. Needless to say the list in his journal grew as more and more kids were added to it.

Over time, more visits ensued and his acts of service grew. He could often be found baking treats in the kitchen with his mom, or making soup and sandwiches for his new friends. This mom spoke of a time when they were out shopping and stumbled upon an incredible shoe sale. Her son managed to persuade his parents to buy the entire stock of sale shoes ranging in size from 7 to 14, for his homeless friends—their van was overflowing!

As Aaron got older he organized bus trips in December and at Easter for his homeless friends to come to his church for dinner and drama presentations where many met Jesus. All were saved from unbelievable situations, some even turning themselves into police because they were on the run and came to realize they needed to confess and do their time in prison! Over a period of four to five years, 86 homeless youth met Jesus as Aaron's "little prayer journal list" grew. "Prayer, unconditional love, and acts of service and kindness always win over judgement!" this proud mom shared, as she reflected upon the beautiful journey they took together.

Hanging on her every word, my cup, still full of coffee, was now cold. With tears trickling down our cheeks we allowed the sacredness of the moment to settle—deeply impacted and changed by a small boy's "venti-sized" heart of compassion.

OUR MOTIVATION

How do we cultivate that kind of compassion in our kids? Acts of service are the hands and feet of our invisible faith. Tangible acts like these, undoubtedly reveal the heart of our Creator to us, our kids and others. How can we weave compassion into the mundane everyday moments of life? You see, I think a lot of this is modelled. Our kids learn what they see. Yet some, like Aaron, will have a natural, God-given bent towards serving others, while others will need to be taught. As parents, that's our cue… we need to prepare the soil; we get to seed it, nurture it and create an environment for it to sprout.

Compassion and serving others are foundational elements in our faith. We follow the One who is known as the Servant King. Jesus gives us the perfect example of compassion, mercy and serving others in Matthew 20:28: *"That is what the Son of Man has done: He came to serve, not be served—and then to give away his life in exchange for the many who are held hostage."*[1] He, the Uncreated One, God of the Universe came to serve us, His created… He gave the ultimate sacrifice—His life for ours. It is that irrational gift that should cause us to erupt in love and service to others.

"Who would you rather be: the one who eats the dinner or the one who serves the dinner? You'd rather eat and be served, right? But I've taken my place among you as the one who serves."[2] (Luke

22:27) Following His lead and His humility, He sets the perfect example for us because He served us. It compels us to respond in the same way.

Jesus profoundly speaks to the significance of compassion and serving others.

Matthew 25:42-45

"I was hungry and you gave me no meal,
I was thirsty and you gave me no drink,
I was homeless and you gave me no bed,
I was shivering and you gave me no clothes,
Sick and in prison, and you never visited."

"Then those 'goats' are going to say, 'Master, what are you talking about? When did we ever see you hungry or thirsty or homeless or shivering or sick or in prison and didn't help?'

"He will answer them, 'I'm telling the solemn truth: Whenever you failed to do one of these things to someone who was being overlooked or ignored, that was me—you failed to do it to me.'"[3]

This is one of the many things I love about our faith and our Creator. Everything of God is completely backwards from what we see and value here on Earth. It is like we have been turned upside down. We so easily overlook the sick and the aging. We lean towards making judgments or assumptions about those in unimaginable circumstances. We are quick to dismiss as we look the other way. Yet, on these precious ones is where our Servant King places intrinsic value. We are all created in His image and when we choose intentionally or unintentionally to overlook the marginalized in our society, we foster a civil war within our very soul as our earthly nature battles the heavenly one.

This is our "why", our motivation for compassion, mercy and serving others. Once we know our "why" it moves us to what must be done. This is what we pass onto our kids, this is what needs to be planted and nourished. It is out of His great love for us—His example—that we are compelled to respond to others in the same way. We give to others out of the abundance that we have received from Him. We mirror to others what He has generously shown to us.

OUR ATTITUDE

God doesn't just want our actions—He wants our heart. As a matter of fact, He is pretty clear that our actions in the absence of love are meaningless. He wants our motives and our reason for *doing* to be pure. His desire is that our invisible beliefs manifest themselves in our physical behaviour.

Ephesians 6:7-8 states that we are to "**serve wholeheartedly**, *as if we were serving the Lord.*"[4]

According to Galatians 5:13 we are to "**serve one another in love.**"[5]

1 Peter 4:9-10[6] challenges us to be "**quick**" and "**cheerful**" to give a meal to the hungry and a bed for the homeless. We are to "**be generous**" with what the Lord has given us.

In Acts 2 the believers "**gave to ALL who were in need!**"[7]

This is what our attitude needs to be when it comes to compassion, mercy and serving others. As we adopt this attitude, we begin to impart and cultivate it in our children. Sometimes the Lord asks us to give out of our wealth and sometimes He asks us to give out of our poverty... remember the widow's mite in Mark 12?

> *"Jesus sat down opposite the place where the offerings were put and watched the crowd putting their money into the temple treasury. Many rich people threw in large amounts. But a poor widow came and put in two very small copper coins, worth only a few cents. Calling his disciples to him, Jesus said, "Truly I tell you, this poor widow has put more into the treasury than all the others. They all gave out of their wealth; but she, out of her poverty, put in everything—all she had to live on."[8]*

Whether we feel wealthy or not is beside the point. In North America, those of us who live in a house, are amongst the richest 5% in the world. When the Bible talks about the rich, God's talking about you and I... and we will be held accountable for how we steward what He has entrusted us with. Ask Him where He is showing you to give out of your wealth, and where He is challenging you to give out of your poverty.

WHY IS SERVING SIGNIFICANT?

As followers of the Servant King, serving is an act of **obedience**. Our goal is to become more and more like Christ as He moulds us and shapes us into the fullness of all that He is calling us to. Serving others puts action to the words we speak and brings a credibility and a weight beyond what we say.

Compassion and serving others is the **fruit of our roots**. Jesus came to serve and if we have given our lives to Him, the Holy Spirit lives in us and we too are called to serve. It is how we show love and demonstrate care. When we serve, we honour God. It is a beacon of His love, concern and faithfulness to others. Serving others reminds those that feel invisible or forgotten that they are significant and that they matter. As we serve, we become a conduit of His love and provision to others.

When Hannah and Caleb were in Senior Kindergarten and Grade 2, we were a part of a church small group made up of families. Making our invisible faith visible to our kids and serving others was one of our group's core values. Each family was given the opportunity to collect food in their neighbourhood for the local food bank with their kids. With wagons in hand, Hannah, Caleb and Ella set out with two of our neighbour's kids to go door-to-door collecting for those in need. As they eagerly walked (ran!) to each door, I waited on the sidewalk with Seth in the stroller. Each child took turns ringing the doorbell and Hannah and our neighbour's eldest were the designated "talkers". Caleb and our neighbour's youngest embraced their role as the "smilers" and Ella naturally bounced with uncontainable joy and excitement as they went from house to house. "Thank you's" rang out as each house exceeded the last in generosity. At the end of our 90 minute tour, we had two overflowing wagons, bags tied to the sides of the stroller and kids carrying anything that couldn't be pulled. The kids were flying high as their joy could not be contained, but I will never forget my neighbour's teary eyes as she saw us approaching. Deeply moved by her children's act of service and kindness, she silently helped us load up the van—the weight of her emotion rendered her speechless.

People are watching, and as we serve others because of the way the Lord has served us, it catches their attention and **draws them to the Father**.

HOW?

Where do we start? What are some practical things we can do to begin to grow and nurture all of this in our kids? Tim Huff wrote a fantastic children's book unpacking homelessness called *The Cardboard Shack Beneath the Bridge*. It is a beautiful resource, exploring the struggles and the reality of street survivors in a way that kids understand. It is a great way to start this conversation with your family if you haven't already.

I struggled with finding a place to start with my own kids. I grew up as a missionary kid, so I was quite familiar with the Great Commission and Acts 1:8 which says, *"Be my witnesses in Jerusalem, and in all Judea and Samaria, and to the ends of the earth."*[9] As this was ruminating in my head during this season of exploring compassion and serving, it struck me that perhaps a formula and starting point was actually in this verse. I began to look at serving in those spheres. What can our family do globally? What can we do in our own city? How can we serve in our community? How can we serve each other in our own family? How can we serve others in our church community? Clarity began to emerge as the fog dissipated.

Globally
Adopt a Child

When Hannah was six years old, she was profoundly moved by the images she saw in World Vision TV commercials. Initially, I would change the channel because I didn't know how to explain such terrible things to a six-year-old. But it was like a magnet to her... if a plea was on TV she was drawn to it. I tried to explain hunger, disease, famine and war to a child who had no context to understand it. She was deeply bothered and deeply troubled by it. As another plea appeared on TV one morning, she looked up at me and emphatically announced, "See, this is what I want for my birthday—to adopt one of these kids!" This bothered her enough to evoke a response... which was a pleasant surprise. Her desire was to use whatever money she received for her birthday towards sponsoring a child. Because of her passion, it ignited a family—ours. Each time one of our kids turned 7 they asked for money to support a Compassion or World Vision child instead of birthday gifts.

World Vision Catalogue

There are many opportunities for us to get our kids involved in serving globally. Organizations like World Vision have other programs, like their Christmas catalogue, that make serving others tangible to kids. One year when their catalogue arrived I left it on the table as the kids came home for lunch. They eagerly flipped through it circling all that they wanted to buy. They presented me with their wishes and while *I* could have bought them, I decided not to. I wanted them to begin to learn about cost and money. I wanted to see if they would still want to do this if it cost them something. We have always given our kids three gifts for Christmas: something they need, something they want and a surprise. I told them they were welcome to choose something for someone else if they gave up one of their presents. Without hesitation all three responded with a resounding "Yes!!" I thought that this proposition might deter them... oh how encouraged I was to see Jesus at work in my kids' hearts!

Operation Christmas Child
Filling green and red shoe boxes for children all over the world at Christmas time is another fantastic family opportunity for kids to serve globally. Kids love wandering the aisles, choosing gifts and selecting treats to fill a box for another kid just like them.

Missions and Missionaries
See what your church is already doing globally and explore the possibilities of having your family join with them in projects they are already a part of. Talk to your kids about the missionaries you or your church supports and create care packages to send them.

Our City/Community
Backpacks
Another initiative that our family small group partnered with was to fill backpacks with pyjamas, a stuffy, and comfort items for kids brought into foster care. Often when kids are removed from a home, they leave with the clothes on their backs. This was an incredible opportunity for kids to serve kids. That year over 100 backpacks were collected, and each recipient was prayed for by a child eager to serve.

Water Bottles and Granola Bars
In the city we live in, we regularly see those who survive on the street. Sometimes it is hard to know how to respond and what to model for our kids. We started packing water bottles with a granola bar taped to it, to hand out. This gave us a tangible way of responding as our kids learned to look them in the eye, hand

them a bottle and say "Hello."

Other Ideas...
- Collect food for the food bank, or toys for a toy drive.
- Buy socks, mitts, and hats for a local shelter.
- Pick up some sleeping bags or blankets for those sleeping outside.
- Contact the local women's shelter, find out what the needs are and fill them.
- Create mini gift bags for the elderly at a nursing home.
- Put together gift bags for street survivors.
- Ask your children's school administrator if there are any kids who need winter gear and fill that need.
- Make some cookies or a meal for a family that is going through a hard time.
- Do yard work for a single mom or an elderly person.
- Let your children choose someone they can be a Secret Santa to.

Our Church

It is important to teach our kids to watch and see, to be observant to the needs around them. Like the movie *Robots* puts it, "see a need, fill a need." They are never too young to start! Initially, it may be reminding them to tidy up the toys when they are playing at someone else's house, or to put their dishes away. Simple acts transition into bigger ones as they get older.

Dear friends of ours walked through a tough season as the mom, who was diagnosed with cancer, received a bone marrow transplant. In our desire to care for and support them, compassion became tangible and practical needs were brought to the forefront.

Cleaning teams cared for their home, gift cards and gifts came in as physical reminders that their church family was with them. "Familying" this dad and his son, with a weekly meal, now home became a practical way of extending the experience of family to them in this difficult time.

Ideas for Serving Our Church Family
- Provide a meal for a family who is sick, struggling or in transition.
- Leave a gift card in someone's mail folder.
- Ask a pastor what the needs are for some people in your congregation and fill them.
- Find out who could use some help with household projects or lawn care that your family could help with.
- Order a surprise pizza lunch for the staff at your church.
- Leave a note for someone who could use some encouragement.

Family
Reflecting on my own family and serving, I started to see how quick I was to help someone else, but I wasn't always quick to help or serve those under my own roof. I am not going to get into all the ways you can serve your family, but I do want to remind you to keep your serving in balance. If we don't extend compassion and service to our own kids, or if they get lost in all the "good" things we are doing for others, we unintentionally overlook our primary mission field—our kids.

One way we began to serve each other was to implement a "secret act of service" day. We each drew a family member's name from a jar and we would surprise the person we selected by secretly doing one of their chores or tasks for them. Sometimes we would change it up a bit and tuck a secret love note into someone's bag or bedroom telling them what we valued most about them. Other times it was about spending time together, like inviting a sibling to play with an older sibling and their friend or doing something special together.

Special Occasion Opportunities
There are so many wonderful spontaneous opportunities to display care, compassion and to serve others. Here are just a few…

<u>40 Acts of Kindness</u>
Mark a 40th birthday or another milestone by spending the day implementing acts of kindness as a family.

My dad suddenly passed away 19 days before my 40th birthday. Draped in shock and grief, we were all trying to process what had just happened. Long before this event, I had planned to mark my 40th by doing 40 acts of kindness with my family. We invited my mom to join us as we embarked on our first family celebration without my dad. Dropping off a pizza at a random person's home for lunch, throwing handfuls of change in our local park for kids to discover, delivering 40 roses to a seniors residence, and writing encouraging post it notes on the Walmart change room mirrors, will go down as one of my most memorable days. In the midst of sadness we experienced a gift none of us could have predicted, as healing, joy and laughter bubbled to the surface. As our focus shifted from our circumstances to the lives of others, restoration started to take place. Each time we came home that day, I was embraced by cards and gifts that friends had randomly dropped off for me. As we were going about our day doing our

40 acts of kindness, dear friends were doing the same for me in the form of gifts and cards filled with words of affirmation and encouragement.

 Free Gift: Forty Acts of Kindness.
Go to: leannecabral.com/book-resources

Shoe Box Birthday Party
For a kid's birthday party, pack shoe boxes for Operation Christmas Child as the activity. With guests in tow, allow your little shoppers to buy gifts and treats for other kids the same age and stage as them. Once back at home, decorate the boxes, pack them up and enclose a little note with a picture for each recipient.

Gift Bags for the Elderly
I know another family who instead of exchanging gifts for their daughter's birthday, asked each guest to bring some spa items for the local nursing home. They provided all the gift bags and some extra treats, while the guests assembled and packed up care packages. Together they delivered them, visited with the residents and painted nails for anyone who was interested.

Street Survival Pack
For their daughter's 13th birthday, a different family decided to gather survival items for youth living on the streets. Each guest was asked to buy specific items instead of a gift. At the party they assembled the packs and left them with friends who work with street survivors.

<u>Sleeping Bag Engagement Party</u>
Friends of ours asked that in lieu of gifts for their engagement party, if each guest would bring a brand new warm sleeping bag to be given out to the homeless.

GIVING AND RECEIVING

As much as many of us are drawn to filling a need and the joy and excitement we feel, two years ago we found ourselves in the position of receiving. James is our sole income earner and was suddenly laid off. The company declared bankruptcy and his severance never materialized. We were a paycheque to paycheque kind of family and we had no income that year, from the end of September until the week before Christmas. The Lord provided so incredibly through the gifts, generosity and care of others during that season. We never went into debt—how is that possible? We regularly talked with our kids that if God can keep Israelites fed and watered and cause their clothes not to wear out for 40 years, than our situation was not above His skill set. We all learned to look for daily manna.

This season, though humbling and hard to receive, was pregnant with lessons and teachable moments. One evening a few weeks before Christmas I received a call from a man who I had done some work for a few years ago. He wanted to know why we hadn't told him about our situation. He then proceeded to tell me that he and his wife decided that they would be our kids' Secret Santa that year and that they wouldn't be buying the "cheap stuff." He informed me that they wanted our kids to know that when things are tough, God cares and He is generous. That Christmas, my kids were dumbfounded, blown away by the irrational generosity of a stranger as they unwrapped brand new iPad minis and a WiiU.

God's extravagant provision is unmistakable in desperate times! Our greatest gift was watching our kids anticipate, recognize and celebrate the daily provision as well as the outrageous over-the-top gifts. Faith became tangible for them—His provision, indisputable. His Faithfulness and care was almost too much to embrace!

Ideas and opportunities to serve others are abundant. As we intentionally seek tangible ways to make our invisible faith visible to our kids, serving is one of the most overt ways to do that. Our kids will copy what they see. They will respond to the seeds sown and begin to scatter a few of their own, too. As we cultivate and nurture those seeds by giving our kids opportunities to practise compassion and serving others, those seeds ripen and sprout. This will cause others to notice, inspiring them to compassion and acts of service too, and ultimately drawing them closer to the Father who knows them by name.

EMBRACING THE GIFT

A Moment to Reflect

- What is stirring within you after reading this chapter?
- How is your family already serving?
- What are some things you could do to encourage serving in your family?

Chapter 12

Family Devotions

Volume crescendoed as our dinner came to a close. Cups were empty and dinner was consumed or scattered on the floor. This tablescape wouldn't make the cut for any design magazine or decor blog. Peas sprinkled the table like confetti, while mismatched, multi-coloured plastic plates and cups anchored the kids' homemade placemats covered with their favourite photos and stickers. With a clean cloth in hand, I began wiping faces and hands as James reached for the children's devotional Bible. Seth began to push his weight back against the highchair and let his body go limp, trying to escape the straps that held him captive. Ella scooted closer to Caleb, encroaching on his space, much to his dismay. He rejected her affection and not-so-gently moved her back with his left arm as she began to pout. Hannah stated her opinion about something and was obviously quite inconvenienced by what was about to happen next.

James pressed on and began to read the devotion for that night, trying to engage the kids with the brightly coloured illustrations and the fluctuations of his voice. I refereed the clan with stern looks, quite possibly some finger-wagging and the strategically placed hand on certain children as they began to lose it. James wrapped up, asking a few questions and said a quick prayer before all that was coming to a boil, fully erupted.

I wasn't sure how this experience and the others that followed would make a difference. I knew family devotions were important and needed to be modelled. I knew it was another opportunity to point our kids to Jesus, but I wasn't convinced that anything was sinking in other than my frustration. Would they begin to associate irritation and frustration with spending time with Jesus?

I grew up in a home that did family devotions after dinner too. I remember giving my parents a hard time about it, although I am confident my insurrection was more internal in nature. Why are family devotions so difficult? Why is it so hard to set time aside as a family to be with Jesus?

The title of this chapter alone can send some people off the deep end. What is it about family devotions that causes some to shudder, others to shy away, and yet another group to rise up and shepherd? This term is loaded depending on what your experience with this subject has been. For some it brings back awkward memories of their own childhood. For others, they shy away feeling ill-equipped to lead their family in this way as they just don't know how. For others still, it evokes joy and a call to action as they embrace the thought of shepherding their family in time with the Lord.

The purpose of family devotions is to set apart time as a family to be with Jesus. No matter where you fall in these previously stated categories, my desire for you is that this chapter brings a little bit of healing as we unpack it. May you feel a tad more qualified and equipped as we debunk some assumptions and simplify things a little. For you who already feel this desire deep within your soul, may you be encouraged with a few more tools tucked away in your belt as you propel your family forward.

DEVOTION

I love where Mark Holmen begins on this topic in his book *Take it Home*. He starts with a question: "What does the word devoted mean?"[1] As you look at the definition or a thesaurus, words like loyalty, dedication, faithful, commitment, attachment, zealous and steadfast come up. What is it that you are devoted to? What do you have a loyalty or dedication to? What are you zealous about? What or to whom are you attached or committed? These are all great questions that help us understand what we are devoted to… or at least, what we think we are devoted to.

My question though, is this: What does our behaviour reveal about what we are devoted to? It is important to know if our behaviour matches up to our thoughts.

What we are devoted to often mirrors back to us through our calendar. What we are committed to, make time for, and spend time on, is all entered into our calendar. The more devoted we become to something, the more time we spend on it or with it. Where do you find most of your time is spent? Time, as mentioned earlier in the book, is like money—we have both variable and fixed time. Most of us can't change our fixed time like work or school, but we do have some choice as to how we spend our variable time. Look at how your variable time is spent. What is your calendar reflecting back to you? Are your thoughts about what you are devoted to and your behaviour aligned?

WHY FAMILY DEVOTIONS?

Obedience
Deuteronomy 6:4-9

> *"Hear, O Israel: The Lord our God, the Lord is one. Love the Lord your God with all your heart and with all your soul and with all your strength. These commandments that I give you today are to be on your hearts. Impress them on your children. Talk about them when you sit at home and when you walk along the road, when you lie down and when you get up. Tie them as symbols on your hands and bind them on your foreheads. Write them on the door frames of your houses and on your gates."[2]*

We set time aside as a family to spend time with Jesus because He directs us to. This time is about teaching our kids about who God is and what His Word says. We are told to impress it upon our kids as we sit, when we walk, when we lay down and when we get up. That is a lot of "impressing!" Notice though that all of this happens as we go about our daily tasks. It is about weaving in God opportunities, God sightings, God moments, as we do our regular, everyday things. This instruction was not meant to be burdensome. It was given as a safeguard, so that our kids would know and remember who God is and His incredible love for all of us. It was given to us as parents to help us make sure our words and behaviour are aligned and in sync.

Community

Lately, I am struck by how God propels us into community. Most of us are happy doing our own thing, managing our own relationship with God as we sprinkle church in here and there, but I think we miss the value and significance of community. Have you ever noticed your own need to "do it yourself" or your own fear of "not wanting to be a burden?" Both our want for independence, which this world places extreme value on, and our own fear of being too much, keep us out of community.

What I think that we forget is that we are made in the image of the Almighty God who in His very nature is three in one. He is the Father, He is the Son, and He is the Holy Spirit. God in His very nature is community and if we are created in His image, we too have a built-in longing, a need and desire for community that we muffle by embracing the lies of "independence" and not wanting to be "needy."

Family devotions, setting time aside as a family to meet with Jesus, is a microcosm of church community. Family devotions are about seeking the Lord together as a family and cultivating a family's relationship with God. Just as individuals have callings on their lives, so do families. Family devotions are about setting aside time together in family community to seek Him.

Remembrance

We set aside time as a family to remember, reflect and recount. We so easily forget the amazing things the Lord has done for us. Reading Scripture is a great way of remembering and reflecting upon that. Another way to remember is to look back as a family and recall when the Lord has shown up in your family's life. Not only does this cultivate gratitude and thanksgiving, it can become a tangible reminder of His faithfulness, His presence and His provision when times are tough.

I wrote earlier in the book about a jar of rocks at our house that we call our "Remembering Rocks". They are a physical representation of the times the Lord showed up in our family. Things are written on these stones like "Caleb's birth" or "Free trip to Disney". Every so often we take out the jar and recount our family stories of God's provision and faithfulness to us. Caleb almost died at birth. He was too big and his shoulder was stuck on my pelvic bone. He was wedged in there pretty good. It was too late for a C-section and the options were slim, either break his shoulder bone or he would be stillborn. A nurse jumped on top of me and began pushing (whaling) on my stomach! Between my pushing, her punching, the doctors pulling and God's providence, Caleb emerged—healthy and breathing.

Our kids regularly expressed their desire to go to Disney. We knew that the financial odds of that happening were not in our favour, so we encouraged them to pray about it and see what would happen. Three years later, we walked through the entrance gates of the "happiest place on Earth!" Emotions were uncontainable, spilling out through my eyes and the squeals of four littles who were about to experience nothing short of a miracle. An older colleague of James' was very fond of him—he had a soft spot for him. He gave us his timeshare in Florida for two weeks one summer when he wasn't planning on using it. We were thrilled as we planned our route down to Florida and all the car activities for four small kids. A week before we were to leave, James received an envelope of cash from this kind colleague—the exact amount for a family of six to go to Disney!

Most of us will remember acts of God like these, but what about the smaller ones? The ones when a pair of leather boots suddenly appeared at your door one day when you needed them. What about the ones where God saves your kid from an allergy you weren't even aware they had? We so easily forget the small things in light of the urgent problems in front of us. We must document the Lord's intervention in our lives, not only to cultivate gratitude but so that we can be reminded of His provision and faithfulness when things look bleak.

Rhythm

So much about what we do as parents is modelling the ebb and flow of life. We play, we rest, we go out and we come home. We have friends over, and we play as a family. We make a mess, we clean it up(ish). The desire to start family devotions when our kids are young is to build time with God into the rhythm of their lives at an early age. Whether it be at dinnertime, nap-time or bedtime, family devotions is about carving out time in our schedules to gather as a family to spend time with Jesus. Our end goal is to raise kids who will take responsibility for and nurture their own spiritual walk when they are old enough.

We get to model what family devotions looks like to our kids. We model what setting time aside looks like. We show them by our behaviour, our attitude, our words and our activities during this time so that they, at the right time, can manage their own quiet time with Jesus.

HOW DO WE DO THIS?

This is the question, right?!? This is where I got stuck, because I could only do what either my parents did or what my limited capacity to be creative would allow me to do. Here are some thoughts that made sense to me when I began to explore this.

Be Flexible – Sometimes what we envision or what we create things that we think are brilliant—just don't translate over to our kids. It can get lost on them. Be willing to adjust and readjust your activities as needed based on how your kids are responding.

Think Outside the Box – If around the dinner table isn't working for you, try outside, in the car or in a different spot in the house. Maybe a special blanket to sit on gives your kids boundaries as to where to be. Perhaps your kids prefer to learn about God through play instead of through a book. Act it out or recreate a story with toys. What about Bible trivia games? Our kids loved learning that way. We even played the Play Station Bible game as part of our family devotions. You get to set up the parameters, so be creative. Your goal is to get them engaged, interested and wanting more.

Keep it Short and Simple – You want to leave your kids wanting more. When they are small, two to three minutes is about all they can handle. As they get older and their attention capacity changes, you can extend it. Most of us can recall devotional times from our own childhood that went on way too long. I think we are better off being too short than too long. This time isn't about communicating complex truths—keep it as simple as possible. Communicate or talk about one concept.

Balance Fun and Focus – So often we get really serious when we speak of spiritual things. Our kids love to laugh and play, and actually, so do most adults! Keep this time balanced between fun and focus. More important than the content you want to teach, is simply the fact that you spend time regularly focusing on God. You are modelling setting time aside.

Persevere – Family devotions may always be a battle for some families. Don't forget we are not only battling kids and moods, but powers and principalities that adamantly oppose what we are trying to do. This is one of those times when as the parents, we know what is best and so we need to push through the opposition both physically and spiritually for the greater goal… the greater good. Don't give up, don't be discouraged. Opposition is usually a good indicator you are headed in the right direction. Even planes take flight against the wind.

Involve the Kids – The more your kids feel a part of the process the more they will take ownership of it. Ask them lots of questions, let them have a say in how this time is spent. Give them choices. As they get older let them lead or plan family devotion time. When our kids were little, as a way of getting them involved, they took turns choosing the activity we would do during our family devotion time.

IDEAS OR ACTIVITIES FOR FAMILY DEVOTIONS

This was the substance I was looking for in tangibly seeking how to pass faith on to our kids. I didn't feel I had enough resources within myself or my history to know what to do during these family devotion times. Interestingly enough, many of the activities I am going to share with you, I shared earlier in the book. They are ones that I had initially tried individually with my kids that I morphed into family activities.

Soaking – Let your kids find a physically comfortable spot, dim the lights and let worship music play. Talk about what they liked about the music, what they felt, what they were thinking about and words they heard.

Dancing – Let your kids choreograph dance moves or actions to their favourite worship songs. Talk about what the song is saying and how to express that physically. Find out why they chose that song.

Computer – Life.Church, JellyTelly and Focus on the Family-Kids, are just a few websites that offer great activities and fun for families, while exploring spiritual truths.

Electronics – There are all kinds of computer games and apps available for kids allowing families to play together while learning Biblical foundations.

Board Games – Bible trivia games are a fun alternative too.

Bible Stories – Some families love reading together, others prefer to act out the Bible stories. Some kids enjoy using props and toys to retell a story.

Traditional – Don't underestimate the power of reading God's Word and praying together. Some use traditional Bibles, others find kids' Bibles more appropriate.

Art – Use art supplies to draw during a soaking experience to express thoughts, emotions and images. You can do the same after reading a Bible story. Have a family prayer journal or gratitude journal to write or draw in as a family. Use art as a medium to explore truths and concepts of God. What does God's love look like to you? When God says to forgive others, paint what that looks like.

Remembering – Have a jar of stones, or pieces of paper that you write on each time God shows up in your family. You are going to need these to recount the stories of God's provision for your family. They become the tales of your family's unique faith story.

Our family devotions have changed a lot over the years. We have had to keep modifying things and adjusting to our kids' growing interests, attention spans and attitudes. We began to incorporate their spiritual pathways (Chapter 9) as they began to emerge. Some devotional times were the perfect image we all imagine, while many others required humility, confessions and apologies as real-life situations collided during our times together. Both the picture-worthy times and the messy ones tell an authentic story of a family's journey to seek God together in the good, the difficult and the turbulent. We are committed to meeting together and seeking the Lord as He continues to weave the faith story of our family together.

EMBRACING THE GIFT

A Moment to Reflect

- What is stirring within you after reading this chapter?
- What have your personal devotions looked like over the last while?
- What are your thoughts and fears around family devotions?
- What are some things you are already doing to set aside time as a family to be with Jesus?
- What are some things you would like to try, to encourage family devotions?

Chapter 13

Talking to Our Kids about Sex

The sun kissed a fiery red goodbye to another day as evening blew in. Children were bathed and in fresh, clean pyjamas, reaching for their toothbrushes before they headed off to bed. James prayed and read with the boys as I tucked the girls in. The light was dim as Ella tried to read her book on the bottom bunk. I crawled up the first few rungs of the ladder to kiss Hannah good night on the top bunk, when she candidly asked, "How does a baby actually get in your stomach?"

"Oh Lordy," I whispered under my breath as I said a quick prayer—glancing down at Ella who was captivated by her book. "Do you really want to know?" I asked.

"Yes," she emphatically replied. I only asked her that question to buy myself a few more minutes to think before I broke this conversation down for a seven-year-old.

I began to explain how God makes our bodies in a special way. I told her about why God's best plan is for babies to be born in the safety and security of a family. We spoke about eggs and seeds and about parts that come together to make this happen. She looked satisfied. I asked her if she wanted to know what parts come together… "Yes," she eagerly replied. So I told her. "That is disgusting!" she announced, as if she had just thrown up in her mouth.

I went on to tell her that is exactly what she should think at this point... but in time and when she gets older it won't seem gross anymore. Knowing my own child's need to speak truth, I reminded her that I am telling her this so that she knows the truth and if she hears anything different—let's talk about it. I also suggested that she keep this information to herself for now—that it was a parent's job to tell their kids this information, not hers. She conceded.

I was quite surprised at how easy this conversation went down. It was smooth and calm—actually quite logical and much of it just seemed to roll off my tongue with ease. I hadn't planned for this conversation, but I could feel the Holy Spirit's quick answer to my prayer as this conversation unfolded with age-appropriate information and language that I hadn't really thought of before.

Even as I write this chapter, I struggle... I think as parents we all want to navigate this topic well. Most of us don't want to relive our childhood conversation about this with our parents. We want to do it better, and yet I am sure our parents wanted to do it better than their parents too. I am not sure James and I have navigated this well, quite honestly. But in my quest to figure out how to pass faith on to my kids, I wanted to know more about how to have these conversations with my kids in a way that made sense and was God-honouring—so here we go...

WHERE TO START?

There is no better person to have this conversation with your child than you. No one loves them more, and no one knows them better and cares more about their well-being than you. You are their best source for information.

Value of Parents

We have to understand our significance as parents when it comes to this topic. We get to **lay the plumb line of truth** and give our kids the information they need to make good choices around their sexuality. We don't want to abdicate this privilege to anyone else—not school, church or peers. We want to get in there and lay the foundation of truth before anyone else does.

We get to choose what we model to our kids. If you are married, **model marriage well**—show tenderness and affection in healthy, appropriate ways in front of your kids. You want them to see and know that marriage is good, desirable and something to look forward to. When was the last time your kids caught you kissing or saw you holding hands?

Our Daughters

Moms, our daughters are watching what we do and say. We must show them how to love themselves by how we love ourselves. Watch your body language and what you say about your own body—she is listening. Be aware of what you say around food and body image. If we want our daughters to dress appropriately, we will need to model that in how we dress. We want our daughters to lean into their uncertain moments and begin to discern for themselves. When they say things like, "How does this look?" and you feel like it isn't appropriate, put the question back in their court with, "what do you think, sweetheart?" We want to empower and equip our girls to practise making these kinds of decisions. Our goal is for them to learn to monitor themselves and trust their choices in what they want to communicate through their dress. Our desire is that our daughters would know deep down inside that they are loved and have intrinsic value. It's our privilege to remind them often of their inherent worth and their remarkable beauty both inside and out.

Dads, you play a significant role in your daughter's life. Though her changing body may be awkward and uncomfortable for some of you, push through it—it hasn't even crossed her mind that this might be difficult for you. Your love for her expressed physically, emotionally and verbally needs to remain constant and consistent. Embrace her and love her the same way you did when she was four. Date your daughter, show her how she is to be treasured and how precious she is. She needs you to show her how she is to be treated so that she will use you as a measuring stick for every other man to match up to. Dr. Linda Neilsen reports: "Regardless of their age, daughters who have meaningful, comfortable relationships with their fathers are generally more self-confident and independent, have better relationships with men and are less depressed, have fewer eating disorders and drug and alcohol problems, and achieve more in school and work."[1] Dads, don't ever underestimate your significance in your daughters' lives. You are a big deal!

Our Sons

Moms, our sons need us to teach them how to date. Caleb and I were sitting at Starbucks one wintery evening. He had his small hot chocolate, overflowing with whipped cream, cupped in his hands as I had my skinny vanilla latte in mine. Sitting in front of the window we watched the snow falling outside. I was doing my typical "1000 question special" when it suddenly struck me that I was the one doing all the question asking. I was the one directing and controlling the conversation. He wasn't asking any questions and it occurred to me that I am going to have to teach him the art of conversation. Though he was only eight, I realized that I need to teach him how to date. We began to play a game of "you ask me a question and I'll ask you one." He quite liked this game and over time a game turned into normal, effortless conversation. He had to be coached initially but he has become a great question asker. He has learned to be observant and ask pertinent questions. He has become an attentive listener as we have continued these dates together even though he is old enough now to take a girl out on a date himself.

Dads, the numbers are hard on you. In their book, *Preparing Your Son for Every Man's Battle*, Arterburn and Stoeker report that "the average father spends about 30 seconds a day in direct conversation with his children."[2] I wonder if for some men the example modelled to them by their own father was lacking. Maybe they didn't have a great example to emulate, so when it comes to having these conversations with their own kids they might feel ill-equipped, and maybe a little fearful or inadequately prepared. More than likely your kids are not going to volunteer information—you are going to have to go searching for it by asking the questions and building conversation into your "hangouts." "Dad has to be close enough to his son to be able to call the *heart of the man* out of the boy. If this does not happen, the next window of opportunity for a young man to try to feel like a man is through his emerging sexuality. So, if dad isn't there early in adolescence to help answer questions, the boy will use his emerging sexuality as an area to answer his questions about being a man."[3]

If we look at Scripture, I think a man is defined as someone who hears God and responds in obedience—a very different definition than the world's. We want our sons to be God's man… not a man's man. Dads, spend time with your sons. Build strategic conversations about sex, relationships and everything else into your time together. Be honest and transparent with them. Show them how to love, honour and respect others by how you love their mom.

Boys and Girls

I think we all agree that there are innate differences between boys and girls, but I just want to highlight a few things in this particular season in their life. During adolescence our daughters must know their intrinsic value and worth. Their self-esteem and self-worth are deeply connected to how they view sex. "Sex is powerful and one of the most manipulated subjects in our culture."[4] Our daughters need to know and understand that they are created for so much more than just the physical gratification of someone else. Our daughters have to recognize the lie our culture promotes— that what is most valuable about her is her body. They also need to understand the power of allurement, how it can be used in positive ways, and how it maybe manipulated in negative ways depending on where her heart is.

In this season our sons have an inborn need to prove that they are a man. That is what adolescence is all about as they transition from boyhood into manhood. Without their father's blessing at this stage, they will seek to prove it in all the wrong ways. Dads, you must verbally affirm your son. Let him know that in your eyes he is a man, that God decided before the beginning of time that your son was to be born male. Tell him that there is nothing he needs to do to prove that he is a man, and that you already affirm it and that the issue is settled. Tell him that you see value in the man standing before you and all that you hope and dream for him. Tell him where you see God in his life and the qualities and characteristics he possesses that make him a man in your eyes.

Lies

Our society has embraced some lies about kids and sex and I fear that we may have adopted them as well. Our children are not animals—they do have **self-control**. As a matter of fact, self-control is one of the Fruits of the Spirit. If the Holy Spirit lives within them, they have the same access to His help and His character that we do as adults. It doesn't mean it comes easy… it takes discipline and practice, but our kids do not have to be governed by their physical or sexual needs. Those needs can be brought under the submission and alignment of God's desires for them. As Pam Stenzel puts it, "if you can say yes, you can say no… it just takes self-respect, character and integrity to say no."[5]

I wonder if we have also bought into the lie that **no matter what, teens are going to have sex** and we have lowered our own expectations of our kids. Raise the bar! Kids need to know their parameters, boundaries and expectations. Set your expectations high and explain *why* it is in their best interest to wait until marriage. Tell them about the cost spiritually, physically and emotionally should they say yes to sex outside of marriage. Our expectations should be aligned with the Father's, who created sex and wants His best for our kids, which includes a healthy, vibrant sex life in the safety and covenant of marriage.

Everyone's doing it seems to be the truth according to what the media is showing and telling us. That just is not so. Not all kids are having sex. There are many kids who choose to be sexually active, but there are many others who for various reasons have chosen to abstain. A study exploring the percentage of Canadian youth age 15 to 17 and 18 to 19 reporting ever having sexual intercourse shows a decrease by 2% over a ten year span. It dropped from 32% in the 15 to 17 age group, to 30% in ten years, and in the 18 to 19 age group it went down from 70% to 68%.[6]

Our Own Sexual History

We need to come to terms with our own sexual history so that we can speak to our kids in an authentic and healthy way. Statistically, one out of four people reading this book has experienced some form of sexual abuse or trauma. It breaks my heart that something that was given to us as a gift has been so abused and perverted. Please pursue your own healing—do not settle for good enough. God wants to be invited into those places too… to bring healing and redemption.

Some of us may fear appearing hypocritical because of our own choices. Know that shame and guilt are an enemy strategy with the sole purpose of silencing you and keeping you stuck from all that God has for you. Invite Him into those places, confess what needs to be confessed. Do not let shame bind you to what has already been forgiven. Our kids have more grace for us than we realize. We don't have to go into detail about our sexual past, but letting our kids know that we have made some mistakes in this area and that we want to help them learn from our mistakes and failures often creates intimacy rather than judgment.

HOW MUCH IS TOO MUCH?

When our kids are little it is hard to know what their little minds can comprehend. I can remember when my guys were small and they would ask questions about where babies come from, I would respond with, "What do you really want to know, sweetheart?" It gave them another opportunity to clarify what they were curious about, and it allowed me to answer the question they were asking, not the one I thought they were. The experts are pretty unanimous in that our kids should be taught the correct names for their body parts. They need to know that a baby grows in a uterus, not a belly. Though nicknames for body parts may be cute, we unintentionally communicate that the correct name is somehow shameful or embarrassing.

James and I decided early on that we would answer any question they asked about babies, sex and body parts with the goal that we would have many little conversations about this, not just one big one. Our desire was to keep this as an ongoing dialogue and that no question was too weird or embarrassing. We knew our response both physically and verbally could either communicate shame or acceptance. We wanted to do this well.

Early one morning with a mirror in my hand and mascara in the other, Caleb looked up at me from where he was sitting and asked, "How do babies come out of a mommy's tummy?" (Apparently we forgot to teach him the uterus part.) I considered answering the four-year-old with the standard, "God helps them out," but quickly dismissed it, because of the concerned look on his face. "Do you really want to know, buddy?" I asked.
"Yes," he thoughtfully responded.

"A baby comes out of their mom's vagina," I replied. He was quiet for a few minutes and I could see the wheels turning as he was trying to process what I just told him.

"How does that work, mom?" he asked, a little perplexed.

"Well," I responded, putting down my mirror and mascara, so I could try and explain this with my hands. "It's kind of like a balloon or an elastic. It expands to let the baby's head and body out and then it snaps back to its regular size." This seemed to satisfy him and I went back to putting my makeup on. A few moments later, a very sincere little voice broke the silence with, "I am really glad God made me a boy."

I think we all want to create an atmosphere in our homes that facilitates these kinds of conversations and the more complicated ones. Answer the questions they ask and take advantage of these teachable moments that often present themselves at the least opportune times.

Another one of my concerns was: how do I talk to my kids about these things, and yet not taint their innocence? Around that time a friend had asked me to review a book for him called *Preparing Your Daughter for Every Woman's Battle* by Shannon Ethridge. I love how she addressed this very issue...

> "Consider for a moment the huge difference between innocence and ignorance. One is a state of heart and the other a state of mind. Educating their mind about this wonderful gift that God has given doesn't remove the innocence that's in their heart nor will healthy knowledge tarnish their sexual purity. If anything their heart will be all the more pure because they will have a better understanding

of God's plan for their sexuality. Scripture says that we are to be shrewd as snakes and innocent as doves (Matt.10:10) meaning we can be both knowledgeable and pure at the same time."[7]

SEX COSTS

The definition of sex has become increasingly blurred over the years, so let me clarify that when I am speaking of sex I am referring to any genital contact including oral sex. Sex in the context of marriage is God's best design for us. It is the safest physically, emotionally and spiritually. He didn't make it this way as just another rule for us to follow, but it is His way of protecting and giving us safety to enjoy sex as an expression of love between spouses. It was God who invented sex, not Hollywood. He created sex for purposes that He determined: "for deep companionship, for filling the earth with children, and for intimate joy between husband and wife."[8] Any time we choose to have sex outside of this context there is a cost and our kids need to know exactly what that cost is so that they can make informed choices.

Spiritually

The act of sex is not only physical, it is also spiritual. Two flesh become one, physically and spiritually. Each time we have sex with another person a soul tie is created with that person.

> *"The Bible doesn't use the word soul tie, but it speaks of them when it talks about souls being knit together, becoming one flesh, etc. A soul tie can serve many functions, but in its simplest form, it ties two souls together in the spiritual realm. Soul ties between married couples draw them together like*

*magnets. In the demonic world, unholy soul ties can serve
as bridges between two people to pass demonic garbage
through. Godly soul ties are formed when couples are
married (Ephesians 5:31, 'For this cause shall a man leave
his father and mother, and shall be joined unto his wife,
and they two shall be one flesh.'), and the Godly soul tie
between a husband and the wife that God intended him to
have is unbreakable by man (Mark 10:7-9). However, when
a person has ungodly sexual relations with another person,
an ungodly soul tie is then formed (1 Corinthians 6:16, 'Do
you not know that he who unites himself with a prostitute is
one with her in body? For it is said, "The two will become
one flesh.')"[9]*

Ungodly soul ties can draw two unhealthy people together like magnets, where their negative traits draw them to each other. The spiritual cost of sex outside of marriage is the creation of soul ties, linking us to our partners spiritually as well as our rejection of God's best for us. Unconfessed sin always places an obstacle between God and us.

Emotionally

A recent study on how casual sex can influence our mental health[10] shows some interesting findings about the emotional cost of casual sex. Participants noted feeling regret about it and that it violated personal standards. Others said that they had significant feelings of regret, disappointment, confusion, guilt and low self-esteem. They noted that they felt positive emotions before and during the "hook up", but felt significant negative emotions after. Other findings showed that people who were not feeling depressed before the encounter felt a significant increase in depressive symptoms, loneliness and higher anxiety after engaging in casual sex. We are built for relationships, we desire intimacy—physically, emotionally and spiritually—and when we pursue sex outside of those safe boundaries where those needs should be met, we pay the price each time.

Physically

The cost of sex outside of a monogamous marriage is most measurable in the price paid by our actual body. If you ask most teens what their biggest fear is about having sex, pregnancy is their number one answer. The problem, however, is that pregnancy is completely survivable, whereas the sexually transmitted infections (STIs) that they come in contact with aren't always. There are over 30 STI's today and 30% of them are incurable. There are two types of STIs; ones that are bacterial in nature and are curable by medication and ones that are viral in nature, meaning there is no medication for them and you will have it for life.

Girls are four times more likely to get an STI than they are to get pregnant. STIs are not equal opportunity offenders—26 damage women, and four damage both men and women. A recent study[11] estimates that there are about 20 million new sexually transmitted infections each year. Young people between the ages of 15 to 24 account for 50% of all new STIs, although they represent just 25% of the sexually experienced population. HPV (human papillomavirus), often referred to a 'genital warts' accounts for the majority of prevalent STIs. One can have the virus and pass it on even though no symptoms are present. The most concerning strain has no warts and is the leading cause for cervical cancer, killing more women a year than HIV. 1 in 4 teens contracts a sexually transmitted disease every year.

I am not trying to scare you, but you have to know where things stand. Most teens do not get tested for STIs. Many STIs are symptomless, so they are being passed along unknowingly. Both Herpes and HPV are skin contacted, meaning you don't even have to have an exchange of bodily fluid to contract them. One in four teens is walking around with 2.3 STIs. Chlamydia is the most common STI in teens and it has no symptoms—you can't treat what you don't know you have.[12]

The chances of our sons and daughters having sex and walking away unscathed physically is statistically unlikely. Their best choice is to make a decision about sex before it is too late. Every choice after that gets more and more complicated along with the consequences that follow. God loves them and wants His best for them, including enjoying sex in the safest place possible—a monogamous marriage where each partner has only had sex with their mate.

CHOOSE HOW YOU WANT TO RESPOND

I think we all want to respond well in a crisis, but most of us don't necessarily know how. Many of us need to see things modelled so that we can emulate it and put it into practice. We know statistically that there is a good possibility our kids may make choices sexually that will have life-altering ramifications. It is hard for most of us to respond the way we would like to in the heat of the moment. So I want you to think about how you want to respond to your kids, should they find themselves in a situation where sex costs.

A few years ago, my dear friend Cathy and her husband Jeff walked this road. Their son bravely told them that he and his girlfriend were pregnant. Cathy and Jeff, who had a very similar conversation with their parents 20 years before, knew exactly how they wanted to respond to this news. Their response was beautiful, sincere and insightful. I asked them to share some tips about choosing our response and this is what they had to say:

- Every baby deserves to be celebrated, regardless of the circumstances that brought them here. Celebrating life is always the right choice. It doesn't mean that you are affirming your child's behaviour.
- Affirm their courage in telling you and not hiding it. Praise their decision to choose life. Cathy shares about the disconnect between words and behaviour when she found herself pregnant at 18. Her family and church always spoke about being pro-life and yet when Cathy chose life, some of her family and church made her feel shamed and judged.
- Focus on your child's positive choices going forward. Watch for new behaviour that is emerging and encourage and affirm it.
- Keep the relationship with your child the priority, not the behaviour. They will remember how you made them feel more than who was right or wrong.
- Be calm and supportive. You don't have to have all the answers—let the dust settle. Find out how you can help and support them—find out what they need from you.

- Be careful of silence. Silence can be shaming and judgmental... even if that isn't your intent. Know yourself and if you need some time to process what you have just heard, communicate that in a way that is honouring and not shaming.

This was their public response to their son, his girlfriend and their grandchild. It was genuine and sincere, but there was also a private side to this conversation that Jeff and Cathy needed to process alone. As much as they celebrated new life, there was also grieving and anger for how their son's choices impacted them. Cathy talks about her wrestle with reputation, even though she knew her son's behaviour wasn't a reflection of her parenting. Both Jeff and Cathy were very aware that this side of the conversation was private and theirs to process. They did not want to speak judgment or shame over their son, his girlfriend or over the new life growing. They worked through this part of it, privately.

Jeff and Cathy spent years having small conversations that paved the way for this one. They addressed the hot topics around sex, pregnancy, drugs and alcohol with their kids and how they would respond. Their kids knew that it was safe to reach out for help when they needed it. They talked through all the "what if" scenarios so that should there be a crisis, their kids would know to reach out to them.

PRACTICAL TIPS

Stall Respectfully
When your kids catch you off guard with their questions, take a moment to pray and ask for help. Ask them a few questions like:

- What do you really want to know?
- Are you sure you really want to know?
- What do you think about that?

This will not only buy you a few moments to think, it helps you answer what they really want to know. It also gives you some insight as to where your child is at or what they believe to be the answer.

Get Feedback

Once you have shared with them, help them process what they have heard by asking questions like:

- What do you think about that?
- Do you have any other questions?

This will help them articulate back to you what they heard and what they understood. It reveals to you if anything needs to be clarified or explained differently. It also encourages further dialogue.

Prepare

Discuss issues and subjects with your spouse first before they come up with your kids. You want to make sure you are both on the same page when it come to topics like dating, masturbation, birth control and certain vaccinations.

Teachable Moments

Between the tyranny of the urgent and the fast-paced lives we lead it is easy to miss opportunities that naturally present themselves around this topic. Our desire is to have many mini talks as well as some longer ones about sex, changing bodies, relationships and marriage with our kids. Ask the Lord to give you practical opportunities to have these talks with your kids and to help you recognize the teachable moments as they come.

Exit Plan

In order for our kids to make wise choices around their sexuality we must equip them with an exit plan. I think they, like us, want to make good choices, but in the heat of the moment when blood is pumping and bodies are responding the way they were created to, it becomes increasingly difficult to do so. Song of Songs in the Bible talks about "not arousing or awakening love before it so desires." "There is a time to awaken and arouse love and the natural act of love is sex. But love and sex are not always synonymous. They are separate acts entwined well in a marriage context."[13] A decision to not have sex must be made at home, before the date... dance... car ride or any situation our kids find themselves in. Our kids need to know and understand what appropriate physical contact is and why. We need to talk about respect, values and boundaries and communicate consistently about them. While opposites may attract in personality, they never attract in terms of character, values and respect for yourself. Help your kids create a plan to exit in case they find themselves in a situation they need to get out of.

Practical Preparations

As our kids embark on this new season of adolescence there are some things we can do as parents to help ease their transition:

- Create a survival period pack for your daughter, a makeup bag with a pad, panty liner, tampon and clean underwear in case her period comes when she is out.

- Create a code word for your kids. A word that they can use if they call you from school or a friend's house, that communicates "get me out of here" without having to actually say that when others can hear.
- James and I have always told our kids to use us or blame us if they need to get out of a situation—"My parents won't let me do that" or "My mom said I have to come home."
- Teach your kids to do their own laundry and sheets before they hit puberty. That way if someone suddenly needs to wash their sheets, no one feels embarrassed.
- Sometimes our kids actually don't know how to have a conversation or get out of a heated session with their boyfriend or girlfriend. We need to talk them through it, beforehand, and give them the language to use so that they feel prepared and equipped.

Sex is a loaded word and having conversations with our kids about it, often leaves parents feeling inept and a little bit fearful. Sex is a significant part of our lives as adults and in my quest to figure out how to live out my faith before my kids in a tangible authentic way, I wanted to address this part of our lives, too. Our kids need to know their worth and value. They need to understand God's desire for them and why boundaries have been placed around sex for their protection. We must talk about the cost of sex and create a plan with our kids, so that they can honour their character, values and those they hold dear when things get blurry. Parents, we also have to create a plan for how we want to respond if or when our kids mess up.

This season with our kids can feel rather vulnerable. Know that you are deeply valued and needed, especially when our kids' behaviour says the opposite. Do not underestimate the power of bringing your kids before the Throne of God in prayer. The same Holy Spirit that lives in you, lives in them if they have given their lives to Jesus. Pray for the Holy Spirit to affirm our kids when they are making wise choices and to make them feel unsettled when they aren't. Laying down the plumb line of truth about sex is one of the greatest gifts you can give your kids. Ask the Lord to give you courage, wisdom and discernment. You can do this!

EMBRACING THE GIFT

A Moment to Reflect

- How are you feeling after reading this chapter?
- What are your fears around this subject? Bring them to Jesus.
- Are there any steps you need to take or conversations you need to have?
- What are some key things you want to remember?

Chapter 14

Money, Allowance and Tithing

I have put this chapter off as long as I can—it may not fall at the end of the book once it's all said and done, however it is the final one I am writing. I have consciously or unconsciously postponed this one as long as possible. Why, you ask? Because we just haven't done this very well in our family. We have fought and wrestled with our finances. We have soared, glided and taken some nosedives. Though I know this seems to come easier for some, we have navigated our finances through trial and error.

Researching this topic was fascinating to me. The experts really do make it sound like common sense—so simple. And as I read their material, I had to agree—it is. How is it, then, that fog seems to descend like an early spring morning, between the reading of it and the implementation of these seemingly simple strategies?

In many ways, I would like a mulligan—a "do over" of sorts. If I could go back in time, I would do things differently with my kids. I would make different financial decisions. "They" say, though, that it is never too late. So, know that I write this with great hope and expectation—hope that my kids can still learn from our errors, and expectation that they can get a solid grasp on money sooner than we did. Hope that they can use their money as a tool to accomplishing God's purposes in their lives and in the lives of those around them.

I also have an incredible sense of hope and expectation for you, dear reader, as we unpack this subject together. Clarity and direction will unfold as you begin to nurture these qualities and characteristics in your own family. For those of you who already have a solid financial foundation, may this chapter encourage and strengthen you as you continue on the path you have laid out. For those who would like a second chance, my hope is that you too will be encouraged—that it is never too late to write a new chapter for your family!

In my mind, this subject falls into two large categories: the attitudes we want to cultivate in our kids and the action we want to ignite. We must understand our own internal beliefs about money, what we do with it and why. Whether we let it manage us or we manage it. It's about embracing the truth that it all belongs to God and He has loaned it to us for His purposes. We have to sort through these things ourselves before we can pass it on to our kids.

ATTITUDES TO CULTIVATE

Our Example

Like so many other things, our kids are watching us and their attitude about money is caught as well as taught. If our belief around money is that there will never be enough we will pass scarcity thinking onto them. However, if we come at it from a place of faith and trust, we can pass on a legacy of faith from a mindset of abundance; that regardless of our circumstances, with God there will always be enough. The same principle applies to our perspective. If you think that you always get the short end of the stick, the lens you view life through will confirm that you always get the short end of the stick. However, if you decide to look at things differently, the lens you choose to look at life through will reflect back to you something very different. We get to choose what lens we use.

Our kids are witnessing how we use our money. They are listening to the language we use around finances. They observe what we spend, what we save and what we give away. Our words are meaningless if the things we say don't match up to what we do. What attitudes do you want to pass on to your kids around money? What language are you using when you speak about finances? Are the things you say and your actions aligned?

It doesn't take much for financial disaster to unfold. As Mary Hunt says in her book, *Raising Financially Confident Kids*, "Take a financially ignorant person, add attitudes of entitlement, and expose him or her to the availability of credit—Ka boom!"[1] Our best move as parents is to choose to do whatever it takes to instruct and guide our kids around money and the significance it plays in our world. Society is eager to teach our kids about finances, needs, wants and entitlement. It nurtures consumerism and materialism in our kids from the time they are old enough to watch TV. If we don't get in there and cultivate Godly beliefs around money first, the world will.

Stewardship
Matthew 25:14-30 tells a parable about a man who was going

on a journey. He summoned three of his servants and entrusted them with his wealth. He gave five bags of gold to one, two bags to another and one bag to the last. When he came back to settle his accounts, both the first and second servant were thrilled to share that they had doubled their investment. The last servant however, hid the money to protect it, and gave back to his master the exact amount he was given. The master was disappointed and rebuked the servant for his poor stewardship of what he had been entrusted with.

Everything that we have comes from somewhere and if we follow that road back as far as it can go, we will see that it all comes from God's loving hands. Whether it is our time, our natural and learned abilities, our personality, our strengths and weaknesses, our talents, our spiritual gifts or our money, they all come from a loving God who has given them to us. They are on loan to us from Him and we are responsible to care for them and use them wisely. Essentially, we are managing God's things for Him—also known as stewardship. According to Larry Burkett, in his book *Money Matters for Kids*, "To be a good steward, we first need to understand that the things and abilities we're managing aren't ours. They don't belong to us, they are God's. They are just on loan. We need to commit ourselves to managing and using them the way the owner (God) wants us to."[2]

We want to be good stewards of all that God has entrusted us with and when we are able to cultivate this attitude in our kids, we begin to lay a solid foundation. One that is built on the understanding that it is all His anyway and that we are responsible to manage it wisely.

Contentment

In a world that is bombarding us with all that we need and must have, and all that we deserve, it is becoming increasingly difficult for parents to fight for contentment—let alone grow that in our kids. Dave Ramsey in his book, *Smart Money Smart Kids*, says, "If you can foster a spirit of contentment in your children while they are under your roof, you purchase the best insurance policy that they will win at life and money as adults. A content person can save, budget, avoid debt, handle relationships and give exponentially better than someone who struggles with discontentment."[3]

Contentment isn't just about learning to live without. It is about choosing to trust God no matter the situation. Content people don't just settle, they begin to look at life through a different lens, making the best out of each situation. Contentment is an internal attitude, a choice that isn't dependent on financial wins and losses. It rests in a settled assurance that God is in control and will care for us.

The demise of contentment begins when we start to find identity in our things instead of in God and how He sees us. We let our status, car, clothes or purses tell us and others about our worth instead of God. This is a slippery slope that will have you sliding full speed ahead into discontentment. This becomes an insatiable appetite that can never be satisfied, gratified or fulfilled.

How do we recognize the collapse of contentment in our own lives? It often starts with jealousy and envy. We begin to covet, wanting what others have. Jealousy quickly moves to restlessness as people begin to worry about all that they don't have. See how quickly our focus can move from God (contentment) to others (envy) to self (worry). We must recognize this pattern so that we can root it out before it begins to spread. Contentment cannot be cultivated in this kind of soil. We must recognize these patterns in ourselves before we can equip and nurture contentment in our kids.

Trusting God

It is imperative to learn to trust God ourselves, in order to pass that on to our kids. Not only trust Him by what we say, but in how that plays out in our behaviour. The funny thing about trust or any other character trait is that it can only be cultivated in trial. There really is no need to trust God when all is going well and we can provide for all of our own needs. That muscle is stretched in opposition. It matures under pressure. It strengthens when things look bleak and we have no other choice than to cling to the One who calms the storm with His voice.

How do we trust Him? We must come from the foundational truth that He loves us, He cares for us, and wants His best for us. Scripture tells us that He has plans for us—good ones that He prepared in advance for us to do (Jeremiah 29:11). The One who is all-powerful, all-knowing and always present is the author of our story and He is trustworthy.

We also need to know what Scripture says about money and respond in obedience when He asks us to do something. We must do things His way and trust Him with the outcome. I heard a story the other day about a man who had five dollars in his pocket. He really felt like the Lord was asking him to give it to a woman he saw in the church foyer. He wrestled with God, since five dollars is a rather small amount to give. Thoughts went through his mind about how he was planning to go out for lunch with his friends after the service. He eventually made up his mind and gave the woman the money. With tears in her eyes she thanked him saying that she knew she needed to be at church that morning to worship and be encouraged, but she only had enough gas in her car for a one-way trip. His five dollars would get her back home. They embraced and parted. His friend came over to him after church, inviting him for lunch. He responded that he'd pass because he already spent that money. His friend laughed and responded, "No, I am inviting you out to lunch as my guest—I have got the bill covered."

We must learn to trust God and have it be evident in the things we say and do. That is the only way we can cultivate that same trust in our kids.

Generosity

I love how Larry Burkett defines generosity as "being willing to give up some of our wants and desires to help meet the needs of others. We can do this cheerfully when we remember God owns everything. He will make sure we are taken care of."[4]

There are lots of places and organizations to give to. Many times we get to choose where we would like to help and sometimes God very clearly tells us where or to whom to give. The best way to cultivate generosity in our kids is by modelling it ourselves. Bring them into your giving conversations.

One family I know decides where they would like to give each year at their annual family meeting. Another family grew giving in their children by asking them each Christmas who they would like to give a surprise gift to. The kids would discuss and choose. Their parents would contribute a significant amount of money and each child was expected to give some of theirs too. Each Christmas Eve, they would drop a surprise envelope full of cash to an unsuspecting person. This is something each child eagerly looked forward to every year. These kids all have kids of their own now. Not only does the original nuclear family still collect money and give, each child has begun to implement this tradition in their own families too. These are some great examples of how to grow generosity in our children.

Another opportunity to cultivate generosity in our kids is to let them be a Secret Santa to someone else. Kids love the anticipation of selecting and dropping off surprise gifts. It also teaches them about the value of giving anonymously.

Generosity is contagious and it spurs others on. Your generosity will inspire your most important audience—your kids.

ACTION TO IGNITE

When we cultivate these attitudes in our kids' hearts, it naturally begins to flow out into their behaviour. It will ebb out in how they manage their own money, and how they plan and budget. It will also affect how they view tithing and giving, along with discerning needs and wants. They will begin to form their own thoughts and feelings around debt and entitlement.

Each family needs to determine their own thoughts and values about finances, specifically around giving, saving, spending and debt. For us, it makes sense to give back first, because we come from a position that everything we have comes from God. Saving is important and it is wise. Our desire is to only spend what is available. The problem with debt is that it puts the loan holder in the position of control and power. While there may be some times that we have to borrow, our goal is to pay off debts as quickly as possible and to avoid being in that situation to the best of our ability.

Allowance

I find there is a great debate amongst parents around allowance. Some tie chores to allowance and others feel that chores are part of being a family community where all help out with things that need to get done. I think we have found some middle ground on this one. We strongly believe that chores are part of being a family, however if there are extra chores that you would like to do above and beyond the ones you have been given, we will pay you for it. We have a chore jar and the kids are welcome to choose a slip of paper with a chore and the monetary value of that chore is written on it.

A jar or envelope system for their allowance money is a tangible way to organize and teach the basics of budgeting. Give each child a set of four jars. Label one *Giving*, another *Long-term Saving*, the next *Short-term Saving* and the last *Spending*.

- Put 10% of their allowance in Giving
- 10% in Long-term Saving
- 40% in Short-term Saving
- and the final 40% in Spending.

Long-term savings are the big things, like college, a car or a laptop. Short-term savings are for things like a new game or an item of clothing. Saving teaches our kids the value of delayed gratification, patience, responsibility and healthy pride.

Larry Burkett breaks spending down like this: "Spending isn't wrong and saving right. Saving is just delayed spending. Knowing how to spend is important and there are three general rules:

1. We don't have to buy anything.
2. When we spend, we spend wisely—ask God first.
3. We don't spend everything right away. We plan to spend a certain amount and we stick to our plan."[5]

You may also want to have a contract with your kids about their allowance and expectations. Have a conversation about where their giving money goes. Find out what they are saving up for long-term and short-term. There may be some things that they are now required to pay for. In the contract a friend of mine wrote for her daughters, her girls were responsible for buying their own socks and underwear. Another family decided that if their kids wanted to go birthday parties, the kids would either have to pay for the gift themselves or a portion of it. Clarity is key—our kids must know the expectations in order to thrive.

Budgeting/Planning
Creating simple budgets for our kids is about equipping them to care for their money in a way that is God-honouring. It should start off really simply like the giving, saving, spending plan mentioned above. Customize the percentages to the unique needs of your family. The only one that Scripture is pretty clear about is the 10% tithe. What we want to communicate to our kids is the value of a plan and that the money coming in must match the money going

out. Having our kids deposit money in long-term saving teaches them the value of dreaming, planning and working towards a goal.

Emmitt Smith profoundly stated "It's only a dream until you write it down, and then it becomes a goal."[6] Mary Hunt, has some interesting thoughts about the importance of a **written plan**. "Our kids' financial futures shouldn't be floating around in some dream state, they must be written down. That way it becomes visually symbolic, it creates authority, it organizes ideas and values. It will also give your kids something to show their kids (think family heirloom)."[7]

Help your kids begin to articulate their own values around money—giving, saving and spending. Write down their goals and update them when they come into fruition or if they change. It becomes a journal that documents their financial choices, hopes and dreams.

As parents we walk a fine line between **grace and legalism** when it comes to teaching and equipping our kids. "Rachel Ramsey tells a story of a woman who had a 10-year-old who was saving up for a gaming system. He had finally saved up the full amount and headed off to the store with his mom to get it. When he got to the cashier, he realized that he had forgotten to plan for the taxes. He left the store empty-handed as his mom was adamant that he pay for the entire system on his own."[8] While she was holding to her "lesson," she may have missed an opportunity to reward his incredible discipline. At 10, he saved up $300 and that is no small feat for a kid.

Sometimes in our desire to teach a principle, we hold on to it so tightly that we miss an opportunity to teach the principle of grace, receiving an undeserved gift that affirms hard work and discipline. As parents we get to decide what lessons we want to teach. Hold your lessons loosely, and be open to the promptings of the Holy Spirit as to which principle He wants your kids to experience. Too many rules are legalistic, but too much grace is enabling. Ask the Holy Spirit to help you walk this fine line.

Sometimes it's hard for kids to **determine needs and wants**. They can look similar, especially to kids. Mary Hunt has some great practical advice around helping our kids figure this out. "Have your children answer this question: What if I could have everything I want? Have them make a list of all the things they would have if they could have everything they want. Next, they need to answer questions such as, Where would I keep everything I want? How would I make sure my things are safe and secure? How would I enjoy all of these things? It doesn't take long for children to understand that having everything they think they want can ruin their lives. They need to know that:

1. Needs are essentials, wants are optional.
2. It is not wrong to want things. Just remember that your wants will always exceed your means.
3. A true need is never realized while you are in a store. If you really needed it, you knew that before you left home."[9]

Tithing

Does God really need our money? Truthfully, no He doesn't— He already owns everything. But it really isn't about the actual money. We tithe and give our money for our sake, to remind ourselves that we are God's stewards and that everything belongs to Him. Tithing becomes a physical demonstration as to who our God is. In the Old Testament other nations brought their money and sacrifices to appease their gods. As believers we freely give our money to God as a physical act declaring that God is our God above all other gods. We tithe because it is a witness to others that all we have belongs to Him. We tithe as a way of offering thanks for how He has so generously provided for us.

Larry Burke defines the tithe as a "tenth in thanks to him for everything, a thanks party because being obedient is a celebration. A way of saying 'Wow God! You are so good.'"[10] Tithing is the tenth the Lord asks us to give back to Him. A tithe isn't limited to money, we can give of our time, talents and treasure. Giving, however, is something we do out of our spending money. It is outside of the 10% tithe. It is money we were going to spend on something else that we choose to give to someone or an organization.

Grandparents

We are so grateful for grandparents and the influence they have in our kids' lives. However sometimes grandparents can unintentionally undo some of the things we are trying to teach our kids. When too much is given too often, it can interfere with what parents are trying to impart to their children. I love how my parents handled this. They decided that for Christmas and birthdays they would give a significant amount of money toward their post-secondary education, their long-term savings. They would also give them a smaller gift or some money to spend on their wants or desires too. They unknowingly honoured and solidified the exact principles we were working to instil in our kids. You may want to have a conversation with the grandparents about the values you desire to pass on to your kids and invite them to partner with you.

Debt, Plastic and Patience

I think *debt* is our most dreaded four-letter word. Here is the problem with debt—it enslaves us to the lender. We lose freedom to choose how we will spend our money. We are bound to those who have the authority and power to collect the debt. As long as we have debt, we are tethered to the loan holder.

Debt always costs us more than we ever want to pay. Not only in interest, but debt steals joy too. With credit so easily available to us, we don't really have to wait for anything. We are becoming accustomed to immediate gratification. We often buy to fill a need only to discover that this thirst cannot be quenched. We try to pacify with things a place that only Jesus can fill.

Debt limits us—it limits our choices, our options and our freedom. We suddenly find ourselves in the passenger seat and debt is driving, choosing where we go and what we can and cannot do. It smothers dreams as quickly as it restrains options. As debt increases, options and choice decrease.

Each family will have to decide for themselves what their stance is on debt. When we save money, God is in charge—when we rack up debt, the lender is in charge. While we may allow our kids to decide how they want to use their spending money, they may need some supervision. Think about whether permission needs to be granted before they go out and buy something.

We also need to be clear with our kids about **borrowing** from us.

Though this may seem harmless now and then, we are essentially giving them free credit and luring them into the same trap that ensnares many of us. Though it may seem harsh, perhaps we need to have a "no borrowing" rule. If you don't have it on you, you can't buy it.

I wonder if **entitlement**, ours and our kids, is what entangles us first? When we begin to buy things because we think we deserve it, we sabotage our finances and the tools we want to pass on to our kids. We have to recognize entitlement when it shows up. One of the best ways to battle entitlement is to change our gaze. Entitlement comes from a place of being unsatisfied. We begin to look horizontally to those around us and feel like we deserve what they have. We take our eyes off of God and His desires for us. The best way to combat this is to start giving stuff away. It changes our gaze from seeing all that we don't have, to seeing needs that we can fill. Staying away from malls and limiting our viewing of advertisements and commercials will also help to refocus our eyes on what really matters.

Money is important and our kids must learn how to navigate the ins and outs of it. Money is a gift and stewarding it requires wisdom and knowledge. As parents we have the privilege of cultivating attitudes around money and igniting action and behaviours in our kids. Money is an incredible tool to use in growing and caring for the things of God. Equipping our kids to navigate this with character and discernment is an incredible gift to give our kids— one that done well, literally keeps on giving!

EMBRACING THE GIFT

A Moment to Reflect

- What is stirring within you after reading this chapter?
- What are you doing well with your money?
- What are some things you could do differently with your money?
- What steps would you like to take to cultivate wise stewardship in your family?

Now What?

T his really is the question, right? Now that I have read all of this, what do I do? How do I get started? Where do I begin? Without a decision to change, without a plan of implementation, everything will stay the same and your family will continue to coast through life being tossed about by circumstances and the tyranny of the urgent.

However, this is what I know to be true about you... you picked up this book and read it because you have a longing for something more for your family. You have embraced the challenge of raising your family in such a way that your kids will know who God is and His incredible love for them. You want your invisible faith to be visible and tangible in your home. You want your kids to embrace Jesus the same way you have and you want it to be real, authentic and vibrant. You want to build a legacy of faith in your family, so let me help you get started.

If you have been journalling the **Embracing the Gift** piece throughout the book, you already have the keys to create a plan for your family. If you haven't, take some time and ponder and pray about the questions at the end of each chapter.

In the first section, **The Gift Given**, you will have explored some of your own obstacles...things that may entangle you and keep you from moving your family forward. Being aware of what ensnares you helps you to navigate with your eyes wide open. You begin to recognize familiar traps before they fully engulf you and reroute you. You become wiser to the enemy's strategic moves and see them for what they are.

In the second section, **The Gift Unwrapped**, I gave you some essential action steps to get started. So if you haven't done so already, make a commitment, pray through your home and begin to draft a family mission statement based on your unique family values.

In the third section of the book, **The Gift in Action**, we explored eight different topics you could begin to unpack and implement in your family to one degree or another. Look back over your notes and see what really resonated with you, because that is what you need to start with.

Create a Five year Plan

Choose five to ten tools or strategies that you would like to implement over the next five years. It may not be the whole topic or chapter, but rather a part of one. Each chapter had several activities and/or tools you could implement to cultivate that particular topic. Be specific and choose what activity or tools you will be using. For example you may choose to implement one or two *Hearing God* strategies. Or maybe *Blessing* resonated with you and you may choose to focus on using words of blessing in your birthday celebrations. Perhaps your first goal is to create a family mission statement. Put your five to ten choices in order of importance to you.

Create a One year Plan

Using your five-year plan as a reference, choose one or two activities or tools, you would like to implement in your family this year. Take each activity or tool and pull it apart.

- Action steps—what do I need to make this happen?
- Are there any potential challenges?
- Do I need to set up boundaries, guidelines or expectations?

 Free Gift: One Year Plan printable.
Go to: leannecabral.com/book-resources

Once you have pulled them apart, put a start date by each activity and put it on your calendar. You can use this same process for years two to five as well.

Things to Consider

<u>Choose One or Two Things to Implement per Year</u>

We tend to overload ourselves in our desire to be diligent. If you only choose one or two things to implement, you will be much more successful than if you bite off more than you can chew.

<u>Introduce One Thing at a Time</u>

If you want to begin to implement words of blessing, stick with that for six months. Get really good at it, let it become a habit, part of the ebb and flow of your family, and then start something new. We are working the long game and in order for these changes to stick, we have to introduce them slowly and let them seep into our family culture. Before you know it five years will pass and you will find yourself almost effortlessly doing these incredible things in your family that you never imagined possible because you allowed them to graft into your family unit slowly and consistently over time.

Be Flexible and Fluid

Create your plan, but hold it loosely…hold on to your Creator tighter than your plan. Allow room for the Holy Spirit to move, guide and change things up as needed. Be willing to adjust and make modifications if that is what your family needs.

Expect Opposition

You have an enemy that is strategically working against you. There are going to be challenges, but press on. Persevere because you know that your dream for your family is worth fighting for. Do not become overwhelmed by the battles—you are fighting a war that ultimately has already been won.

Celebrate your Wins

It is so easy for us to focus on what isn't going well, or on all that still needs to be done. Choose your focus and celebrate the amazing things God is already doing in your family. You may need to do this daily or weekly. For others it may be monthly or yearly. Write it down as a living altar of remembrance, one that will remind you of God's faithfulness in your family. It will encourage you and breathe life into weary places when the battle seems to surround you. It will serve as a memoir of the story the Lord is authoring for your family.

<u>Pray</u>

You can't actually do this on your own…even with an excellent plan. You will need God's help and wisdom. This endeavour needs to be bathed in prayer. We are created to be dependant on God and on our community. Invite others to pray for your family as you seek to implement these tool and strategies.

Know that I have been praying for you and your family. My hope is that you walk away from this book feeling encouraged by what you are already doing in your family. That you feel empowered to continue on as you intentionally point your kids to Jesus. May you feel more equipped as you make an invisible faith visible and tangible in your home. May you be excited and expectant of all that the Lord is going to do in and through your family!

May the Lord bless you and keep you and give you great favour. May He give you such insight and joy as you faithfully point your kids to Jesus. May He affirm you as you go. May He bless the plans you have created and give you the desires of your heart. May He give you a glimpse of your impact and influence. According to His Word, He says, *"that He will instruct you and teach you in the way you should go, that He will council you with His loving eye upon you."* (Psalm 32:8) May the Lord give you wisdom and look favourably upon you and your family. May He do immeasurably more than you could ask or imagine! May He continue to build a legacy of faith in the story of your family…and for generations to come!

Just One More Thing...

You may not know that this story of passing faith on is not actually about religion, but about a relationship. Though we explored *A Parent's Best Gift*, God offers you the *Perfect* Gift.

You may not know that God also wants a relationship with you. He loves you and sent His Son to die for you and me, to pay our penalty for sin so that the relationship that was severed by sin, could be made right.

The Bible says, *"For God so loved the world that He gave His only Son, that whoever believes in Him will not die, but have everlasting life. For God did not send his Son into the world to condemn the world, but to save the world through Him."* (John 3:16-17)

If you would like a relationship with God, all you need to do is accept the gift He has already extended to you.

You can pray a prayer like this...

> *Dear God,*
>
> *I realize that I need You in my life. I am tired of doing things my way. From this point on I want to rely on You and do things Your way. I believe that You sent Your Son in my place to die and that He rose again so I can spend eternity with you. Please forgive me for what I have done wrong. I surrender to You. Please give me Your peace and make all things new. I want to follow You and live my life in relationship with You.*
>
> *Amen* (Which means, so let it be.)

Free Gifts

All free gifts can be accessed at leannecabral.com/book-resources

Notes

Chapter 1: Full Bloom Parenting

1. Psalm 78:1-7 NIV.

Chapter 2: Death to Comparison

1. Inspired by Craig Groeschel, #Struggles podcast part 1-5, MP4, accessed October 2014, https://open.church/resources/1938-struggles/.
2. Craig Groeschel, #Struggles part 1, podcast video, MP4, 8:24, accessed October 2014, https://open.church/resources/1938-struggles/.
3. Exodus 20:17 NIV.
4. Craig Groeschel, #Struggles part 2, podcast video, MP4, 7:00, accessed October 2014, https://open.church/resources/1938-struggles/.
5. Craig Groeschel, #Struggles part 1, podcast video, MP4, 25:13, accessed October 2014, https://open.church/resources/1938-struggles/.
6. Craig Groeschel, #Struggles part 3, podcast video, MP4, 26:46, accessed October 2014, https://open.church/resources/1938-struggles/.
7. Proverbs 4:23 NIV.

Chapter 3: Warped Views

1. Isaiah 40:11 NIV.
2. Jeremiah 29:13 NLT.

Chapter 4: Embracing the Challenge

1. Deuteronomy 6:6-7 NLT.
2. Ephesians 6:4 NLT.
3. Proverbs 29:17 NLT.
4. Psalm 127:3-5 NLT.
5. Inspired by Leslie Leyland Fields, "The Myth of the Perfect Parent" Christianity Today, January 2010, http://www.christianitytoday.com/ct/2010/january/12.22.html?start=5/.

Chapter 5: Where Am I and Where Do I Want to Be?

1. Inspired by George Barna, Revolutionary Parenting: Raising Your Kids to Become Spiritual Champions (2007).
2. Dawson McAlister, Finding Hope for Your Home (Irivng, Texas: Shepherd Ministries,1996), n.p.
3. Search Institute is a non-profit, non-sectarian research and educational organization that advances the well-being and positive development of children and youth through applied research, evaluation, consultation, training and the development of publications and practical resources for educators, youth-serving professionals, parents, community leaders and policy makers. Phone: 1-800-888-7828. Website: www.search-institute.org.
4. George Barna, Transforming Children Into Spiritual Champions (Ventura, CA: Regal Books, 2003), p.78.
5. Dr. Phil, "Life Strategies" http://www.drphil.com/articles/article/44.
6. J.P. Morgan, http://www.goodreads.com/quotes/223825-the-first-step-towards-getting-somewhere-is-to-decide-that/.
7. Emmitt Smith, "Hall of Fame speech." ESPN, August 7, 2010, http://espn.go.com/blog/nfceast/post/_/id/16456/emmitt-smith-hall-of-fame-speech/.

Chapter 6: Charting the Course

1. Inspired by Mark Holmen, Faith Begins at Home (Ventura, CA:Regal Books, 2005) p. 23,28,36.
2. Joshua 24: 27 NIV.

Chapter 7: Prayer

1. Matthew 6:7-8 NIV.
2. Luke 18:7 NIV.
3. Cheri Fuller, When Children Pray (Colorado Springs, CO: Multnomah Publishers, 1998) p.58.
4. Inspired by Cheri Fuller, When Children Pray (Colorado Springs, CO: Multnomah Publishers, 1998) p.28, 29, 31, 35, 40.
5. Inspired by Cheri Fuller, When Children Pray (Colorado Springs, CO: Multnomah Publishers, 1998) p.60.
6. Inspired by Cheri Fuller, When Children Pray (Colorado Springs, CO: Multnomah Publishers, 1998) p.72.

Chapter 8: Blessing

1. Inspired by Terry & Melissa Bone, The Family Blessing Guidebook (I.D. Ministries, 2012) p.7.
2. Terry & Melissa Bone, The Power of Blessing (Terry and Melissa Bone, 2004) p.28.

3. Terry & Melissa Bone, The Power of Blessing (Terry and Melissa Bone, 2004) p.29.
4. Proverbs 18:21 NIV.
5. Terry & Melissa Bone, The Power of Blessing (Terry and Melissa Bone, 2004) p.29.
6. Numbers 6:22-27 NIV.
7. Terry & Melissa Bone, The Power of Blessing (Terry and Melissa Bone, 2004) p.3.
8. Terry & Melissa Bone, The Power of Blessing (Terry and Melissa Bone, 2004) p.2.
9. Terry & Melissa Bone, The Power of Blessing (Terry and Melissa Bone, 2004) p.29.
10. Inspired by Craig Hill, The Ancient Paths (Craig S. Hill, 1992) p.28.
11. Inspired by Terry & Melissa Bone, The Family Blessing Guidebook (I.D. Ministries, 2012) p.38,39.
12. Mark 1:11 NIV.
13. John 1:29 NIV.
14. Terry & Melissa Bone, The Power of Blessing (Terry and Melissa Bone, 2004) p.122.
15. Mark Holmen & Dave Teixeira, Take it Home (Ventura, CA: Gospel Light, 2008) p.65-69.
16. Galatians 2:20 NIV.
17. Matthew 5:14,16 NIV.
18. Numbers 6:24-26 NIV.
19. Ephesians 3:17-19 NIV.
20. Packard, Amen Simulcast.

Chapter 9: Hearing God*

1. Brad Jersak, Children Can You Hear Me? (Brad Jersak, 2003) n.p.
2. Brad Jersak, Children Can You Hear Me? (Brad Jersak, 2003) n.p.
3. Brad Jersak, Children Can You Hear Me? (Brad Jersak, 2003) n.p.
4. Acts 10:34 NIV.
5. Jeremiah 29:13 NIV.
6. Gary Thomas, Sacred Pathways (Grand Rapids, Michigan: Zondervan,1996) p.14.
7. Inspired by Gary Thomas, Sacred Pathways (Grand Rapids, Michigan: Zondervan,1996) p.16,17.
8. Jeremiah 29:12 NIV.

* Inspired by a Hearing God workshop created by Beth Graf and Leanne Cabral.

Chapter 10: Spiritual Protection*

1. 2 Timothy 1:7 NLT.
2. Jonathan Thompson, "Spiritual Warfare" (presentation, Tyndale University College and Seminary, Toronto, ON, June 1-5, 2015).

3. Jonathan Thompson, "Spiritual Warfare" (presentation, Tyndale University College and Seminary, Toronto, ON, June 1-5, 2015).
4. Jonathan Thompson, "Spiritual Warfare" (presentation, Tyndale University College and Seminary, Toronto, ON, June 1-5, 2015).
5. Revelation 17:13-14 NIV.
6. Jonathan Thompson, "Spiritual Warfare" (presentation, Tyndale University College and Seminary, Toronto, ON, June 1-5, 2015).
7. Inspired by Charles H. Kraft, I Give You Authority (Bloomington, Minnesota: Chosen Books, 2012)
8. Jonathan Thompson, "Spiritual Warfare" (presentation, Tyndale University College and Seminary, Toronto, ON, June 1-5, 2015).
9. Ephesians 6:11-17 NIV.
10. Ephesians 4:26-27 NIV.
11. "Strong's Greek Concordance." accessed May 13, 2016, http://biblehub.com/greek/5117.htm.
12. Romans 12:18 NLT.
13. James 5:16 NIV.
14. Joshua 1:8 NIV.
15. Zechariah 3:2 NIV (Paraphrased).
16. Acts 2:44-47 NIV.
17. Malachi 3:10-12 ESV.
18. Ephesians 6:13 NIV.

* Inspired by a Spiritual Protection workshop created by Beth Graf and Leanne Cabral.

Chapter 11: A Family Who Serves Together...

1. Matthew 20:28 MSG.
2. Luke 22:27 MSG.
3. Matthew 25:42-45 MSG.
4. Ephesians 6:7-8 NIV.
5. Galatians 5:13 NIV.
6. 1 Peter 4:9-10 MSG.
7. Acts 2:45 NIV.
8. Mark 12:41-44 NIV.
9. Acts 1:8 NIV.

Chapter 12: Family Devotions

1. Mark Holmen & Dave Teixeira, Take it Home (Ventura, CA: Gospel Light, 2008) p.72.
2. Deuteronomy 6:4-9 NIV.

Chapter 13: Talking to Our Kids about Sex

1. Shannon Etheridge, Preparing Your Daughter for Every Woman's Battle (Colorado Springs, CO: WaterBrook Press, 2005) p.52.
2. Stephen Arterburn & Fred Stoeker with Mike Yorkey, Preparing Your

Son for Every Man's Battle (Colorado Springs, CO: WaterBrook Press, 2003) p.5.

3. Stephen Arterburn & Fred Stoeker with Mike Yorkey, Preparing Your Son for Every Man's Battle (Colorado Springs, CO: WaterBrook Press, 2003) p.31.

4. Darlene Brock, Help Wanted (Estro, FL: The Grit and Grace Project, 2011) p.132.

5. Sex-Ed, No screwing around, produced, directed, filmed and edited by Reel Insyte, DVD.

6. "Statistics on Sexual Intercourse Experience Among Canadian Teenagers", SexualityandU.ca, accessed December 2015,(http://www.sexualityandu.ca/sexual-health/statistics1/statistics-on-sexual-intercourse-experience-among-canadian-teenagers).

7. Shannon Etheridge, Preparing Your Daughter for Wvery Woman's Battle (Colorado Springs, CO: WaterBrook Press, 2005) p.13.

8. Ross Campbell, MD with Rob Suggs, How to Really Parent Your Teenager (Nashville, Tennessee: W Publishing Group, 2006) p.132.

9. "Basic Introduction to Soul Ties," Great Bible study.com, accessed December 2015, http://www.greatbiblestudy.com/soulties.php.

10. Susan Krauss Whitbourne Ph.D, "How Casual Sex Can Affect Our Mental Health," Psychology Today, (March 9, 2013.): https://www.psychologytoday.com/blog/fulfillment-any-age/201303/how-casual-sex-can-affect-our-mental-health.

11. "11 Facts about Teens and STD's", DoSomething.org: https://www.dosomething.org/facts/11-facts-about-teens-and-stds.

12. Sex-Ed, No screwing around, produced, directed, filmed and edited by Reel Insyte, DVD.

13. Darlene Brock, Help Wanted (Estro, FL: The Grit and Grace Project, 2011) p.136.

Chapter 14: Money Allowance and Tithing

1. Mary Hunt, Raising Financially Confident Kids (Grand Rapids, MI: Revel, 2012) p.18.

2. Larry Burkett with K. Christie Bowler, Money Matters for Kids (Burkett & Kids, LLC, 2000) p.7.

3. Dave Ramsey and Rachel Cruze, Smart Money Smart Kids (Brentwood, Tennessee: Lampo Press, 2014) p.183.

4. Larry Burkett with K. Christie Bowler, Money Matters for Kids (Burkett & Kids, LLC, 2000) p.39.

5. Larry Burkett with K. Christie Bowler, Money Matters for Kids (Burkett & Kids, LLC, 2000) p.43.

6. Emmitt Smith, "Hall of Fame speech." ESPN, August 7, 2010, http://espn.go.com/blog/nfceast/post/_/id/16456/emmitt-smith-hall-of-fame-speech/.

7. Mary Hunt, Raising financially confident kids (Grand Rapids, MI: Revel, 2012) p.186,187.
8. Inspired by Dave Ramsey and Rachel Cruze, Smart Money Smart Kids (Brentwood, Tennessee: Lampo Press, 2014) p.69.
9. Mary Hunt, Raising Financially Confident Kids (Grand Rapids, MI: Revel, 2012) p.141,142.
10. Larry Burkett with K. Christie Bowler, Money Matters for Kids (Burkett & Kids, LLC, 2000) p.23.

Acknowledgements

Wow, what a ride this has been! I had no idea how many people it would take to produce this book. I am so grateful for the remarkable people and resources the Lord provided. I am acutely aware of how much I needed each one of you. Though your names may not appear on the cover, your stories, impressions, wisdom and prayers are woven into the pages of this book. With an incredibly grateful heart—thank you.

At the onset of this quest, my simple prayer was this: "Lord if you can multiply loaves and fishes, could you please multiply time, ability and capacity for me?" In awe, I watched Him do this time and time again. For a moment this ordinary girl got to do something extraordinary through the power of the Holy Spirit... and for that I am so humbled and grateful!

To my husband, James, you are my biggest fan and cheerleader. There is no one more loyal and steadfast than you. You are home to me. Thank you for believing in me and the message the Lord entrusted me with. Thank you for living out this material with me and our kids!

To my kids, you are the catalyst for this book. Thank you for teaching me how to be a mom. Your unconditional love and encouragement has taught me immeasurably more than I could have imagined and without you I would have never embarked on this expedition.

To my parents, I am so incredibly grateful for the example of faith, obedience and steadfastness you were to me. Thank you for your perseverance and obedience in the big and small things. Your life allowed me to see Jesus and His incredible provision and care! Dad, I wish you were here to read this so that you could more fully know the legacy you passed on.

To my coach, Kary, thank you for your support, enthusiasm and wisdom. Without you, this book would still be a "someday" dream. Thank you for creating a program that walks one through the authoring process from concept right through to a finished product. Thank you to the AAE Tribe for your encouragement, insight and suggestions. You are an inspiration!

To my funders, at the onset of this journey you partnered with me, believing in me and the significance of the message I have been entrusted with. You understood the urgency to "get it out" and you made it possible for me in ways I could have never imagined... thank you.

To my friends and cheerleaders – Amanda, Beth, Cathy, Dawn, Dayna, Doug, Hilary, Jenn, Julie, Kaire, Kim, Lorie, Merry, Rachel and Rose, your faithful encouragement and prayers breathed life into me and this project! Thank you for interceding for me, the book, and the families who will be reading this!

I am so grateful for the team of editors and friends that came alongside me. Amy, Heather, Monique, Nathalie, Nikki, and

Susie – thank you for sharing so generously of your time, gifts and talents! You all were an answer to a very specific prayer!

Sweet Lucy, you are a brilliant artist and a dear friend. Thank you for the breathtaking artwork on the cover and throughout the book! I am so grateful for your friendship and the gift of your talents.

To the Worlds Apart board, Brett, Brian, Brian, Doug, James, Pete, Ryan and Scott – thank you for your support and for all that you do behind the scenes. You are a blessing!

To any whom I may have forgotten to thank or acknowledge, my sincerest apologies… know that the Lord used you and you are valued, even when my memory fails me!

To you, dear reader – I am honoured to be with you and grateful to be entrusted with a few minutes of your time. It is a privilege I don't take lightly! May you feel welcome and at home here, like we are sharing a conversation over a warm cup of coffee. May you walk away from our time together feeling embraced, encouraged, excited and equipped for all that the Lord has in store for your family!

Jesus, I watched you fully fund this endeavour. You provided specific people and resources exactly when I needed them. You truly multiplied time, ability and capacity and I love that I get to tell this crazy faith story of your ridiculously generous provision!

Let's Linger a Little Longer...

Have you ever been fully emersed in a great conversation only to have it cut short? It is so disappointing when that happens and it leaves you longing for more. There was more to say and more you wanted to know. I love conversations that have room to linger.

If you'd like to pour another cup of coffee and linger a bit, we can keep talking—I would love to hear from you!

- Tell me about your family and what the Lord is up to.
- Let me know what you found helpful in the book or what really encouraged or resonated with you.
- What tools or activities are you working on?
- Do you have any modifications or ideas that you would like to share?
- What is working well in your family?

Let's celebrate together!

Facebook Author Page
Join Leanne's Facebook community, "like" her page and feel free to leave a comment.

You can follow Leanne on **Instagram** @leanne_cabral_

You can also find her at leannecabral.com

Bring Leanne
Into Your Organization

Mother~Author~Speaker~Coach

Leanne's passion is to equip parents as they navigate the awesome task of passing faith on to their children. She encourages parents to make their invisible faith visible and tangible so that they can intentionally point their kids to Jesus and build a legacy of faith. Leanne's grace-filled, authentic approach, combined with excellent content empowers parents with tools and strategies that are tried, tested and true. She is happy to tailor her talks and training to the unique needs and desires of her audience.

Contact Leanne today to begin the conversation
leannecabral.com

Made in the USA
Charleston, SC
04 September 2016